Film Design

$3.95/£1.50

In the same
Screen Textbook Series
produced by The Tantivy Press

Compiled and edited by Russell Campbell

**Photographic Theory for the
Motion Picture Cameraman**

Practical Motion Picture Photography

Compiled and edited by Terence St.John Marner

Directing Motion Pictures

Film Design

compiled by
Terence St. John Marner
in collaboration with
Michael Stringer

The Tantivy Press, London
A. S. Barnes and Co., New York

Preface and Acknowledgements

This is the fourth of a series of textbooks which will eventually provide a complete grounding in film production techniques for the young professional film-maker. As in the other books in the series we have relied on the experience of experts in gathering our material. Most of the Designers who have helped us with this book are members of the Guild of Film Art Directors, the professional association to which many of the leading Film Designers in Great Britain belong.

I would like to thank the Guild for supporting my work throughout, and especially I am indebted to those Designers listed at the end of the book, who agreed to contribute to this project. I am also extremely grateful to Michael Stringer who gave initial shape to the book with his many suggestions and who has subsequently contributed Chapter One, in addition to much technical advice in other chapters, and has read the manuscript and written the Introduction. He has worked hard to ensure that the advice contained in this work conforms to the highest standards of the Guild of Film Art Directors.

In addition I wish to thank Madame Lotte Eisner who gave generously of her time to my research at the Cinémathèque Française in Paris during the preparation of the exhibition *75 Years of Cinema*. I would like to thank M. Henri Langlois, Director of the Cinémathèque, for allowing me to photograph many of the exhibits.

I also wish to thank Charles Swynnerton and Julia Palau for their help with proof-reading; and Derek Elley for compiling the filmography of the contributors.

Finally, I wish to thank Mr. E. Smith-Morris for his advice and help in the preparation of the illustrations; Mr. Robert Dunbar, Principal of the London Film School for his continuing enthusiasm for the series; Mr. Michael Hoad and Mr. Stefan Dreja for the excellence of their design; and Mr. Peter Cowie, of the Tantivy Press.

Throughout this book I have used the term Designer to cover the activities of both the Art Director and the Production Designer.

Illustrations supplied by courtesy of Mirisch Film Production Company, United Artists, Walt Disney Productions, Worldwide Films, Winkast Productions, Rank Organisation, Columbia Pictures, 20th Century-Fox, Cinema Center Films, Warner Brothers, and Peter Cowie.

First Published 1974
© 1974 by Terence St.John Marner
Library of Congress Catalog No: 72-9938
SBN (U.K.) 90073069 2
ISBN (U.S.A.) 0-498-01326-X

Printed in the United States of America

for
Dominic and Jayne

Contents

Frontispiece: Light and Texture in John Box's design for *Oliver!*

Introduction

Every feature film is made by the combined talents of many dedicated people, and the film Art Director or Production Designer is one of the key creators of any feature film, whether it be a film shot entirely on location or in the studio. Each shot in any feature film should be designed with loving care, and this desire for perfection is the result of many days, months, or even years of thought by a team of film-makers, and of this team the Art Director is one of the most important members.

The Art Director contributes the vitally important visual background of the feature film. He is an artist who adapts his style to any number of various types of film. He integrates himself and his associates totally into the mood and feeling of the particular film whether it be a comedy, a musical, an adventure, a fantasy, or a very intimate social drama. The range of his material is inexhaustible, the scope of his design is limitless and the Art of Art Direction is to make the imagination soar to seemingly impossible heights within a practical and economic framework. He has to tame his imagination into the hard and fascinating task of making all things physically possible for filming. In his process of re-creating he cannot work alone like an easel painter or a writer, and his work is constantly under the steady fire of time, economics, changes of mind, physical construction and execution and his own self-critical mind and eye. Until his first idea sketched on paper becomes a finished reality he goes through weeks or months of ceaseless doubt, joy, critical analyses, and constant observation of his "brainchild." And like so many creative processes he does not really know how his efforts will materialise until the film is cut and finally assembled and screened to an audience. All through the shooting period of the film the Art Director will be constantly checking and re-checking the movements of the camera, the wishes of the Director and Cameraman, the Producer, the Cost Accountant and his own staff. He will find himself part artist, diplomat, craftsman, at various times of the day, every day, and all the time his eyes will be searching and re-looking at his sets and costumes, and the progress of the shooting.

The Art Director provides the backgrounds and all the time he tries not only to please himself, but the Director first and foremost, and only by close collaboration with the Director can he ensure that his sets are well photographed and contribute to the totality to the film.

In this comparatively new art form called Cinema, film sets have developed rapidly from canvas theatre backcloths to their present highly sophisticated form. The rapid development of film sets over the last few decades has been made possible not only by increased budgets but also by the very high standards of craftsmen who build and make the sets. Film Industry artist craftsmen— the Carpenters, Plasterers, Painters, Riggers, Property men, Signwriters, Scenic Artists, Metal Workers, Drapers, Stagehands, have all contributed a huge amount with their skill, energy and superb craftsmanship.

Each year new developments in construction and visual processes make the building of film sets more exciting, more malleable, and sometimes more economic. All the time the possibilities for new ways of expression are opening out, and in spite of the recurring crises in the industry the film medium still holds its magic and its marvellous potential as an art form and entertainment for millions of people. The Art Director is always looking forward to use every possible means to make the dreams of the film-makers a splendid reality.

Michael Stringer
President,
The Guild of Film Art Directors

Chapter 1
Basic Considerations

This chapter illustrates certain basic aspects of film design.

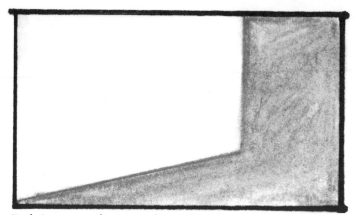

Each image on the screen has: Tone

Contrast

Perspective

12

Focus

Movement within the frame

Colour and texture

The object of the picture

No 1 Plane

No 2 Plane

No 3 Plane

Within the frame there is tone

and texture

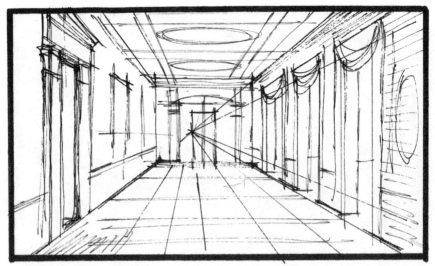

and perspective

and the source of light

Dramatic use of shadow and composition in Eisenstein's Ivan the Terrible.

The use of off-balance in Dreyer's Joan of Arc.

Symmetry

Assymetry

The uses of foreground to give depth.

Making use of levels—steps—ramps—raised levels—balconies—staircases.

The use of the camera angles: Tilt up

Tilt down

Tracking or panning or tracking and panning

Movement is: Either within the frame

or by camera movement: Tracking or zooming.

Panning ─────→ *with an actor or some object*

Tracking and tilting up

or tilting up or down or tilting up and around.

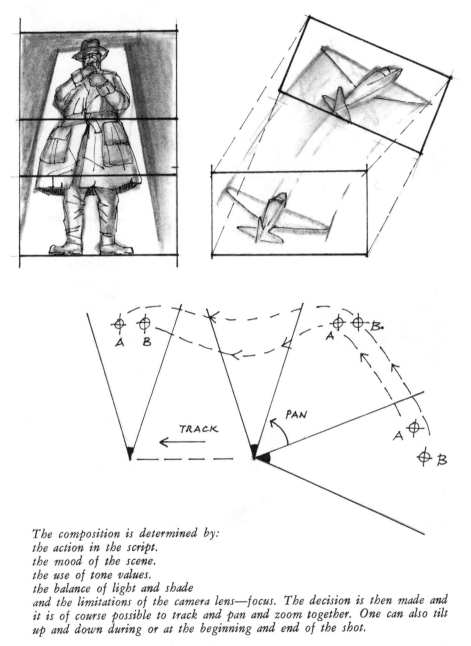

The composition is determined by:
the action in the script.
the mood of the scene.
the use of tone values.
the balance of light and shade
and the limitations of the camera lens—focus. The decision is then made and
it is of course possible to track and pan and zoom together. One can also tilt
up and down during or at the beginning and end of the shot.

The dramatic use of a prop.
The hat cuts off the eyes of the man listening to the other man in the foreground who is reading a letter. From William Wellman's The Ox-Bow Incident.

Split focus from foreground to background.
Split focus dramatically used to indicate the foreground character's lack of interest in the suffering of her poisoned husband struggling up the staircase in the background. Up to that moment in the film (The Little Foxes) *everything had been shot in deep focus. But when the husband attempted to struggle up the staircase the background was kept deliberately out of focus to accent the foreground character's callousness in not wanting to help her husband.*

Some Words of Warning.
Always co-operate closely with the costume designer and unless this is the desired effect either change the wallpaper and chair fabric or change the actress's costume.

Always keep a close watch on the dressings behind or in front of artists, otherwise a plant or tree or a foreground prop will create an effect which nobody will intend.

Always try and stop the artiste's legs from being cut-off in a musical dance number. It is much more effective to see the complete figure in this type of set-up and the Designer can help to persuade the Director, Cameraman, and Operator to set up the camera to make sure of seeing the complete figure.

One has to consider the wide screen cut-off, and the final viewing of the film in the cinema where the projectionist might not rack the projector correctly and the carefully composed set-up can be ruined for the audience.

Chapter 2
Preparation

The blue-print for a film is the script and it is during the first reading of the script that the Designer begins to shape the film in his mind.

"When one reads the script the story content conjures up pictures in one's mind. Sometimes the script clearly describes the kind of location one will need or it might even specify a particular location that one can easily find. The script might also describe the characters fairly accurately, and in one's design one will underscore the characters to make them more believable. This initial visualisation process is not done in a slow laborious way. Rather the mind instinctively conjures up a stream of images during the first contact with the script. During the reading the characters are put in their setting." (*Shampan.*)

It is a help if the Designer can quickly record some of these images as thumbnail sketches. The purpose of the sketches is to provide a record of these first design ideas. They need not be seen by anybody else, but will at a later stage be the basis for more finished sketches.

"When going through the script for the first time I make a great number of thumbnail sketches and pencil notes. This gives me an overview of the whole film. In this reading I will get many ideas for the treatment of the design and I have found that these first ideas are the ones worth keeping. They certainly are the freshest and most original. At a later stage I will select from these spontaneous drawings those which I think should be worked up into more elaborate drawings.

"Paying particular attention to the action I try to visualise where the key events will take place within the set. This reading also helps me to see what are the key points of dressing to keep in mind. For example, there may be a table that will be involved in some way with the action." (*Stringer.*)

The above procedures assume that one is working from an orthodox script. Some films, however, rely more heavily on design content and in the instance of the Bond films the design may serve as a basis for action rather than the reverse:

"The Bond films cannot be seen as examples of 'normal' film-making. When I started on each of them I started with the book and not a script. Before we got to the script stage I, along with a number of other people, came up with ideas that were incorporated into a screenplay. I spent two or three months at Universal studios in Hollywood going through their research library and coming up with ideas that I considered for inclusion in the script. This is not the usual way of designing a film. In *You Only Live Twice* I went off to Japan and found an extinct volcano and thought it would be fantastic to have the villains inside it and this idea was then written into the script. This kind of planning is much more of a collective effort with many people throwing ideas up for possible inclusion. It is rather like a circus—devising what one can do that is more thrilling than the previous stunt. On *Dr. No* we had a number of writers at work but of course nobody was sure of the potentiality of the material. I thought we should give the story a rather larger than life feeling and try to make it thoroughly contemporary." (*Ken Adam.*)

Breaking Down the Action

The action of a film is the catalyst for the design. The design content does not have an existence separate to the movements of the actors—it is not in any way an abstraction. From the beginning therefore the Designer should be very conscious of the action within a scene and at an early stage he should analyse the scene carefully to discover what Jack Shampan calls the *mechanics* of the action.

"Apart from describing the characters of the film or the locations of the action the script also describes the *mechanics* of the action; for example, a character may enter through a door or may exit; or he may go down some stairs. At a second reading which I do very slowly I make little thumbnail sketches describing much of the mechanics of the script. I am not concerned with the *décor* at this stage but just the bare mechanics of the action." (*Shampan.*)

Wilfrid Shingleton describes his discussions with Roman Polanski that took place after the first reading of the script of *Macbeth*:—

"Polanski and I went through the script together and discussed each scene. He then drew a little plan of the way in which he wanted his actors to move across the screen. This helped us design the set for the action involved. For example, when Macbeth and Lady Macbeth are talking about the killing of the King we put them in the foreground and through the window in the background we could see the King in bed. The high level gallery around the courtyard was designed because when Lady Macbeth goes with the sleeping potion in the pitcher to the King's room Banquo comes out with his son and walks across the courtyard. Polanski wanted to build up suspense as the audience is wondering if Banquo is going to see Lady Macbeth. We needed

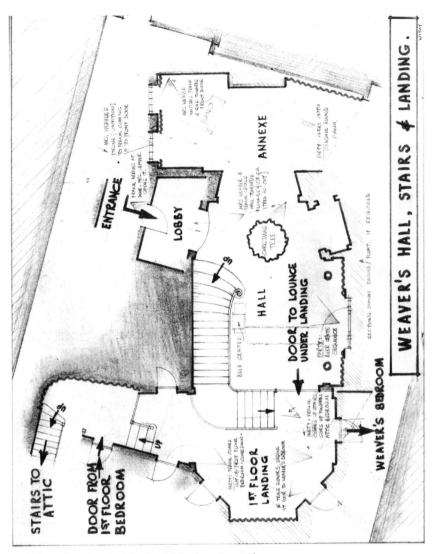

Set plans by Alan Withy for This Sporting Life.

therefore a fairly heavy column behind which Lady Macbeth could hide."
(*Shingleton.*)

The meeting between Macbeth and the witches at the beginning of the film
also created a problem because the action demanded a visual separation between
Macbeth and Banquo.

"'The exterior ruin on the moors was a very difficult set to design because
it has been done so many times. The play calls for a ruined abbey with arches

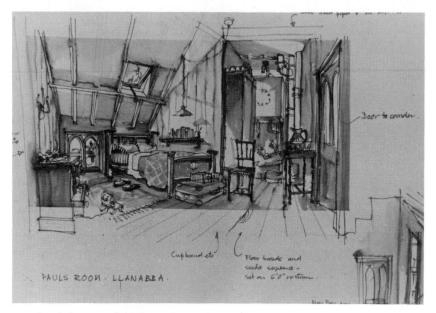

Set sketch by Jonathan Barry for Sitting Target.

and I did some designs on these lines.

"The dramatic essence of this part of the script was that Macbeth sheltered with Banquo and they heard the witches 'off-stage.' Polanski wanted Macbeth to ride off and see the witches and be able to talk to Banquo while Banquo could not see the witches." (*Shingleton.*)

Even in scenes in which there is not a lot of physical movement it is the action, the dramatic essence of the scene, that is the Designer's starting point.

"Everything was designed completely on the action. In the scene in which Lady Macbeth sees spots of blood on her hand with the other group discussing her, I wanted to give emphasis to the distance between Lady Macbeth and the group. Also when young Seaward comes in to kill Macbeth, Macbeth is seated at the end of the hall and I wanted to give the hall a feeling of emptiness." (*Shingleton.*)

Jonathan [John] Barry describes how the design of a staircase in an apartment centred on specific action:

"The room was meant to be in a little mews cottage—a hideaway where a man kept his girl-friend. The cottage had to feel cut-off since in one scene they beat up a man living in the mews without disturbing neighbours. A man gets killed falling down the stairs so the stairs had to look as if one might fall down them and also look as if they might kill anyone who happened to fall down them. The stairs, therefore, had very awkward curves and were tiled with sharp edges." (*Barry.*)

32

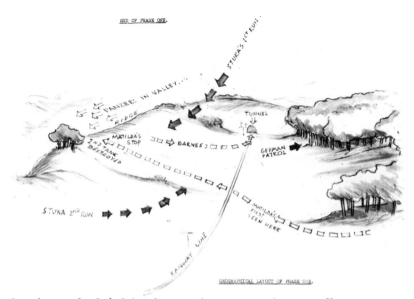

Phase lay-out by Syd Cain of one action sequence in a war film.

Breaking Down the Action in Action Films

Some films are dependent for their impact on broad sweeps of expansive action—war films are perhaps the most representative of this type; other examples are Westerns and historical romances, etc. In these types of film the Designer will have to deal with moving people and perhaps vehicles through large expansive sets. The action may be quite complex as in a battle scene. The Designer has, therefore, more *mechanical* problems to deal with. The Designer in such films may find that before examining the small detail of design he has to come to terms with larger areas of action within each scene. Syd Cain describes how he has broken a war film script into its "phases" of action.

"After reading the script of *The Iron Daffodil* I broke it down into phases. Very roughly the story concerns a British tank that gets cut off by German Panzers about the time of Dunkirk. They have various adventures in their attempt to get back to the British lines. Each adventure I have called a 'phase' and the script is broken into a number of phases. I do this very quickly and roughly. Putting these phases into a visual format always helps the Director and Writer because this visualisation enables them to change the script if necessary.

"In other words, I prepare a little scheme of the various phases of the film. For example, the first sequence of action opens with a German patrol coming through a wood. They reach the edge of the wood and hear the noise of a tank. They see two tanks approaching and go over the railway line—they do this

1

2

3

4

5 *Storyboard lay-out by Syd Cain for* Iron Daffodil (*in preparation*).

so that I can establish a tunnel. They go up to a ridge and then look down from the top. It is a nice peaceful scene until they notice some Panzers; the object of this shot is to show what they are up against. They decide to take cover in the tunnel. As they turn around they are dive-bombed by a Stuka and one tank is destroyed. The hero's tank reaches the tunnel. Just as they get into the tunnel the Stuka bombs the mouth of the tunnel and they are entombed. That is the end of what I call Phase One. I then divide up this action into actual scenes using the script outline as a guide. I work out the close-ups and the medium shots as suggestions for the Director. Finally, of course the shot breakdown is up to the Director but my visuals will give him something to work on. He might change things around drastically but the shots I select are ones that will establish the action clearly for the audience; where the tanks are; how they fit into the location; what is going to happen and how." (*Cain.*)

To a certain extent the Film Designer has to think theatrically. The actors have their entrances and their exits in the film as validly as on the stage, and their action on the set becomes an important aspect of their characterisation. If the Designer allows himself to be carried away by beautiful set sketches that do not relate to the action then it will be impossible for the Director to develop his characters within the prepared set. A table is placed because it is a part of the total integration of the numerous elements that make up the screen image. A table is not placed near a window because the prop men happened to put it there or because the Designer happens to like tables to be placed near windows.

Designing for Character
In addition to the mechanics of the action one also gets the first glimpse of a character during one's first reading of the script. Sometimes the characters are very clearly described by the scriptwriter, perhaps even down to the kind of clothing worn by the characters. In other scripts a character may be much more difficult to define as in the case of Alex in *A Clockwork Orange.*

"Alex's character was a problem in that as a narrator in the book his character didn't have to be as complete as is necessary to a successful visualisation. Therefore, when putting him on the screen we had problems trying to decide what kind of dressing would go with our understanding of his character." (*Barry.*)

Even a character who is clearly defined in the original script can undergo a metamorphosis during the production of the film and this can mean headaches for the Designer who has to continually change the set dressing to keep up with the character emerging from the rehearsal process rather than the script. Again one character in *A Clockwork Orange* develops on the set largely because of the personality of the actress chosen for the part.

"The cat lady was originally meant to be a wealthy old lady who had a lot of cats. She was meant to live in a rather old shabby house. But as the film progressed, and after Miriam Karlin had been cast, the character developed into the one we had on screen and instead of living in the old house in London she lived in a rather fine country house. The exterior shots of the house were of an existing country house and interiors were built in a gymnasium at a physical recreation centre. The works of art displayed in her room were meant to give an unnerving edge to her character and the whole *décor* was meant to make her of indeterminate age. In the book her character is *cliché*—an old lady living with her cats, but in the film she becomes quite unique." (*Barry.*)

Period
One more basic factor that will be an important aspect of the design is the period into which the story has been placed. Films set in the clearly definable past are going to require copious research into costumes, architecture etc., and films set in the future will have their own design requirements, to convey the feeling of future time. Films in which the period is not the present but the near future, or the recent past, create problems, because many of the visual elements in the film will be indistinguishable from many elements of contemporary design. In designing *A Clockwork Orange* Jonathan Barry was met with a situation in which the film takes place changed from far future to near future. He was able to use some elements of contemporary design successfully while other design elements had to give the impression of being in the future.

"As the preparation progressed Kubrick decided that the film need not be set as far in the future as he had originally intended. Indeed, he felt that by setting the film in the near future it would add impact to the story. A film set in the distant future can appear completely set-off from our own time and is likely to be written off as 'futuristic.'

"As the film developed, therefore, the time became more current and we were able to use things like Volkswagen cars on the assumption that their design would not change for a few more decades." (*Barry.*)

Set Planning
The method of analysing the script outlined above is based on the procedure of making a number of rapid sketches which can clarify the action or the character and put the whole into a specific point in time. There is another method of working from the script which is used by some Designers who prefer to see the script as a number of three-dimensional sets rather than a succession of two-dimensional screen images. Scott MacGregor explains his approach to the script in the following way:—

"As a first step I usually work out the plan of the set. Many Directors are quite happy if you present them with a plan which can be modified during your discussion with them. Once a Director is satisfied that everything that he wants is going to be constructed in the right place according to the action he has planned he will be happy to leave it to the Designer to get on with the construction." (*MacGregor.*)

Thinking in three dimensions from the beginning has many virtues. The greatest probably is in forcing the Designer to be completely honest about what he feels able to produce. Some Directors will blame Designers for impressing them with beautiful sketches that have nothing very much to do with the set that is eventually built. Either the Designer is unable to build from a sketch or he is more concerned with impressing the Director by presenting him with the impossible. Most Designers feel that it is a point of honour never to present the Director with anything that he (the Designer) is incapable of producing. The set plan approach is certainly a way for the young Designer to ensure that he does not fall into the trap of producing pretty sketches that do not take in account the three-dimensional problems he has to tackle.

After having his plan accepted by the Director the Designer can then do a number of sketches from the plan. These sketches are a good guide for all

36

A Life for a Life *Two stages in planning a "disco" sequence. A back projection screen is set up for lighting effects. Dark background is provided by black velvet backing. Carpeting effect is provided by coloured hessian (burlap).*

the smaller departments within the art department.

"I then work from the plan in producing a number of sketches that give everybody interested an idea of what we aim to achieve visually on that set. I always get my sketches printed so that one is available for the Set Dresser, the Buyer, the Prop Men etc. The Carpenters also have working drawings of course. This helps them because specific measurements do not matter to me, but cause critical problems to them. When they see the overall effect I am after they can make minor decisions about the size or height of things without always having to refer to me." (*MacGregor.*)

Models

Rather than proceed from the plan to the sketch of a set many Designers will first make a model of the set. Indeed, although some Designers will not produce continuity sketches or detailed set sketches, most Designers make models of the various sets to be built.

For the Director the model has distinct advantages over set sketches. The finished set is obviously three-dimensional and it helps the Director in his visualisation if he can look through a view finder at a three-dimensional representation of the finished set. He can quickly see what he will get using various lenses.

It is a mistake to think that if even a very good detailed sketch is presented to the Director he will be able mentally to translate the information in the sketch into three dimensions. One sometimes hears a Director state that Designers do not give them on set what the Designer originally sketched. This may happen, but it can also happen that a Director may misunderstand what has been shown to him in two-dimension format. The Designer *draws* one idea, the Director *sees* another.

Conscientious Directors will insist on having as much information as possible from which to work. This does not inhibit the Designer, rather it ensures that the Director gets exactly what he wants.

Models can be easily made from cardboard or plywood. In a large production the Junior Draughtsman will execute the work under the direction of the Designer but a Designer will also be able to produce them himself. Michael Stringer remarks:

"Depending on the time available I will always make models of the key sets using a view finder to ensure that what one is building will be a fair representation of what one anticipates on the screen. At this early stage I build to the widest angle lens to get a rough idea of what the set will look like. At a later stage I will, of course, have a more precise idea of the set." (*Stringer.*)

Bird's Eye View Diagrams

A bird's eye view diagram is a quick way of presenting the plan and elevation of a set to the Director. It also helps the Designer to grasp the total concept of the set at a glance. Michael Stringer describes how he set up the bird's eye view diagram in Blake Edwards's *A Shot in the Dark.*

"We wanted to build the set in this rather complex way since there was interlocking action planned between the various rooms. This is a rather more complex set than one would normally have to prepare. There were other sets in which we worked out very elaborate moves of actors and actresses running

Prince and the Pauper *Preparatory model of a period set. Michael Stringer designed some of the buildings on moveable platforms to allow for re-use of some of the buildings in different positions.*

out of various bedrooms, seen from the outside of the house. This plan was not produced as a measured isometric drawing. The drawing was done before the action was worked out. Initially I knew that we had a mansion and I knew the number of rooms as well as the size of each room and its function. I presented the drawing to the Director and he accepted most of it with a few amendments. At a later stage we decided to cut out the dining room and we changed the lay-out of some of the rooms." (*Stringer.*)

Isometric Drawings

An isometric drawing is a true plan and a true elevation set up at a sixty degree angle so that both elevations can be read together. Isometric drawings are very useful in that they can save making a model in many instances.

"I have made isometric drawings on many films, notably on *Genevieve*. Henry Cornelius always liked to see isometric drawings of all his sets so that he could move little cardboard cut-outs around on them." (*Stringer.*)

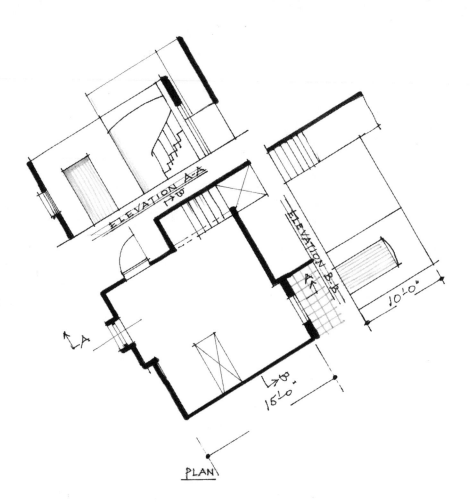

ELEVATION A-A

ELEVATION B-B

PLAN

Making an Isometric Drawing from the Plan and Elevations of a Set
Draw the plan at a 60° angle on the drawing board and set up the necessary
elevations. Trace over the original plan and raise the elevations until one has
built up the true elevations.

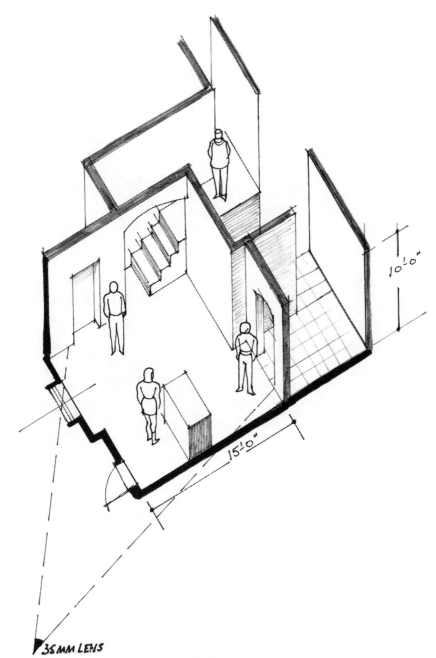

35 MM LENS

All heights are to scale; the plan is also to scale, and one can move cardboard cut-out figures (to scale) anywhere on the drawing. It is a very helpful projection for working out the action of a scene—almost as good as a model of the set.

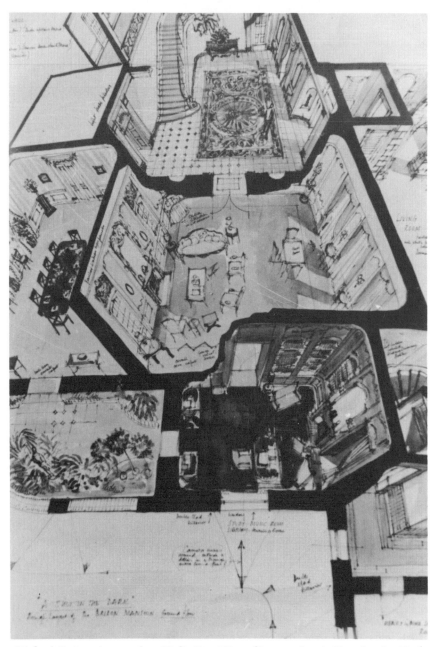

Michael Stringer's complex Bird's Eye View diagram for A Shot in the Dark.

Continuity Sketches

After the Designer has mapped out the broad sequences of action or produced a number of detailed sketches of the main sets it is often useful to the Director to have a sketch of each individual shot. The larger production such as *Fiddler on the Roof* or *Where Eagles Dare* will almost certainly hire a Sketch Artist to produce these continuity sketches. The sketches can be presented as a storyboard as in the example on the page opposite or as a series of detailed sketches that put across the feeling and action within the shot.

"A great number of extremely good continuity sketches were produced for *Fiddler* by Mentor Huebner and John Michaelson in Hollywood. Norman Jewison found them extremely useful as a guide and the sets were designed with the key sketches in mind.

"In various Disney pictures that I have worked on everything has been story-boarded. In these films and other fantasy subjects there is a terrific use of continuity sketches. They are essential in trying up matte shots and effect shots. Hitchcock uses sketches extensively.

"Ideally the Designer will do his own key sketches and then depending on time he will employ a Sketch Artist to work with him and the Director. The Director and the Sketch Artist very often work hand in hand. This is a useful procedure for the Director especially on the bigger production since it helps clarify action and detail. In the case of *Alice in Wonderland* Will Sterling and I sat down every day for three weeks and I sketched every single set-up with him. This is a marvellous way of preparing a film." (*Stringer.*)

John Stoll found the preparation of a story-board useful when planning action sequences in *Cromwell*.

"For action sequences one needs to produce a story-board, although in a film like *Cromwell* there was room for a great deal of freedom. Directors do not like to be held to a story-board but if there is a great deal of action, for example using ships, then one will want to analyse the details of the action well ahead of shooting." (*Stoll.*)

Treatment

After producing the initial sketches or set plans the Designer will have to decide what kind of treatment he is going to give to the overall design concept. The Director will have a big contribution to make in this matter since it will be his interpretation of the script that will determine much of the way it is presented on screen. When preparing *Casino Royale* a highly stylised design treatment seemed to be called for to underline the Bond satire.

"I associated with Joe McGrath in the early days of *Casino Royale*. His idea was a send-up of the Bond myth and we deliberately explored the idea of having mad extravagant Pop Art ideas mixed with the fantasy, Bond, and the rich women with whom he consorted. I did a tremendous amount of research into Pop painting and we devised a number of design gags such as having the top of Nelson's column outside Ursula Andress's bedroom, fish-tanks one could shoot through; miniature baccarat tables in a recess; a sofa well and about fifty feet of Elgin marbles down one wall. We tried to make the whole design *chic* and extravagant in a lightweight way. In her dressing room we put a multitude of mirrors as a pastiche of early Jean Harlow films with the deliberate contrast of Hieronymus Bosch wardrobe cupboards. In the colour scheme of the bedroom we used black, white, pink and grey and generally used cool colours throughout."' (*Stringer.*)

Colour Guide
A colour guide for the whole film becomes essential when determining what is the most appropriate treatment for a theme.

"I always produce a rough colour guide running through the whole film. I work out what tones to use in the different scenes and decide, to a certain extent, what quality of colour I will have—solid colours or atmospheric colour. Getting the colours correct is a matter of interpreting the character of the script." (*Stringer.*)

Finished Colour Sketch
After having had the sketches and set plans approved by the Director and after deciding on the overall colour quality of the film the Designer is then in a position to produce the first finished colour sketches. He will select some of the key sets in the film by virtue of the amount of building and cost or by virtue of the action involved. The sketches will incorporate a piece of action and fairly detailed set dressings.

Shooting Test
Colour schemes should be tested whenever possible and it is usual to use test sets for this purpose. The test sets are built to be used to test actors but it is a good opportunity to try out costumes and fabrics or certain photographic effects. Since one will be able to see the results of the test on screen it is also a good opportunity to try out anything about which one has doubts.

Research
Whatever the subject of a film, the Designer must spend many hours ensuring that the visual detail he will put into the screen images will be accurate. Even though he will have many people working for him it is still necessary for him to have a remarkably wide general knowledge of periods and styles of costume, architecture, the decorative arts etc. His background training for the profession will be an important factor since he may already have for other purposes studied the history of architecture, furniture etc.

"To be a successful film Designer it is essential to have at least some training in an art school, or to have had architectural training. One should have a knowledge of period styles and one should certainly be able to visualise in the style of any particular period. If, for example, one is designing Georgian architecture one will have to understand proportion and have a feeling for it." (*Marshall.*)

In addition, the Designer should know where to find out what he needs to know. He should be conversant with the collection of his local library as well as the libraries in the larger metropolitan centres. Indeed, many Designers have their own reference libraries covering the decorative and applied arts, fine art, and architecture running to a hundred volumes or more collected over the years.

Superb continuity sketches by Mentor Huebner for Fiddler on the Roof *designed by Bob Boyle.*

Procedure

Once again, the script is the point of departure for the entire research period. Designers have their own particular patterns but they all have to relate to the script. The main areas that will have to be covered are:

Locations

Props

Costumes

The principal problems met with in researching locations are described in Chapter Four but one particular difficulty that is perhaps more a matter of intuition than technique, lies in the capturing of mood and the ability to re-create this mood authentically in the studio. Although there are certain technical methods that are commonly used when making a studio reconstruction of a location, much of the success of the Designer will depend on his intuitive ability to grasp the almost indefinable subtleties that make the character of a location so unique. Ted Marshall was in great difficulty in this respect when he had to come to terms with the realities of a northern English industrial town used in *Room at the Top*.

"I have worked a lot on what were known as 'kitchen sink' films, *A Taste of Honey, Saturday Night and Sunday Morning, Room at the Top,* etc. They are concerned with life in the north of England. One finds that after producing one or two films within a particular *genre* one is very quickly regarded as an expert within that *genre*. I am not from the north of England and I think this has been a help. When I went up to Bradford for *Room at The Top* I was really appalled by the environment. Some of my associates on the film saw everything in a very romantic sort of way—the mills, the smoke, the dirt—but for me there was no romance at all. It was sad and desperate. The next time I went back I was returning to something I knew and I had been looking at paintings by Jack Simcock and L. S. Lowry. Gradually, I began to understand that there really was something there." (*Marshall.*)

John Stoll had a similar problem when designing *The Greengage Summer*. He had to create a highly romantic French set that reflected the romantic vision of France of an English schoolgirl. His task was very much a matter of capturing a particular atmosphere that comes not only with a country but a particular part of that country. With less attention to detail one could construct a perfect replica of a French *château* and still fail to grasp that certain quality of its being authentically French.

Props will normally be obtained by the props department but it is the responsibility of the Designer to specify as far as he can what he will need. Again, the Designer should know what he is after and be conversant with as much written or photographic reference material as he can find. Some Designers keep their own library of reference photographs and clippings covering an extremely wide range of subjects. Museum catalogues and professional journals are both good sources of material of many types. When working on the furniture to be used in the author's house in *A Clockwork Orange* Jonathan Barry remembered an exhibition he had seen in a London department store and for which he had the catalogue. This furniture eventually became the basis of that actually used in the film.

Peter Mullins's assignment on *The Last Valley* serves as another useful example, this time in the use of museums.

"Luckily we were based at Innsbruck, where there is the best folk museum

Proposed lay-out by Michael Stringer for Pinewood lot set for The Horse without a Head.

in Europe. They were very helpful and allowed us to photograph reconstructions of period interiors. We were able to use a lot of actual specimens as set dressings. However, we made a lot of the furniture ourselves as copies of originals in the museum. My assistant measured up what we thought we could use—bowls, spoons, platters, jugs etc. We took the full-size sketches along to a local wood carver whom we employed to make the copies." (*Mullins.*)

Michael Stringer comments on some of the problems encountered while researching for *Fiddler on the Roof*:

"During the research period we used the London Library extensively. Bob Boyle (the Production Designer) had already built up a very extensive reference file in Hollywood. We established a vast library of photographs that were in constant use throughout the filming. We even tried to reproduce some of the photographic quality that is peculiar to old photographs.

"Luckily the Yugoslavs still had the steam engines we needed. At one time I spent some time trying to find a similar expanse of snow-covered landscape which hopefully we could have used with one of the many steam engines that one can find in rail museums in Britain. I went as far as Wick in North East Scotland to find a suitable piece of level ground but the snow count was so small that we couldn't take the risk of the snow not falling at the time of shooting because we wanted a snowy landscape." (*Stringer.*)

Research into historical battles requires not only information about costume detail but often period battle formations.

"I did a great deal of research on battles of the period when working on *Cromwell*. I had to know a lot about weapons in addition to the formation of the various armies on the field of battle. On the historical film one has to be extremely precise in detail to make the effect acceptable." (*Stoll.*)

In films of contemporary battles, national war museums (and there is one in most of the main film-making countries) can provide valuable information and examples of contemporary weapons. Acquiring actual cars, or tanks

47

etc., used in battle may be quite difficult but much is still available. Syd Cain describes how he tried to obtain the material that he anticipates using in a war film still at the planning stage.

"I do a breakdown of all the vehicles that I would like. This is sent to various countries in the hope that they will be able to supply at least some of the equipment. I have to spend a great deal of time in libraries and museums after getting the script to make sure that we have every detail correct." (*Cain.*)

When preparing for *Fiddler on the Roof* Michael Stringer hunted for every scrap of photographic material concerned with Jewish communities in the Ukraine and read as much about the life there as possible. Jonathan Barry and Stanley Kubrick went through ten years of all the leading architectural journals selecting a list of buildings that seemed possible as locations for the film *A Clockwork Orange.*

"Kubrick likes to work from as much information as possible. He wanted to set the film in the future and as far as possible he wanted to shoot the film on location because he had a limited budget. I was involved with the film an unusually long time before shooting started and I had time for some very thorough research." (*Barry.*)

On most productions one will have a costume designer who will work with the Designer to ensure that the costumes fit into the overall design concept.

"There has to be a great deal of co-operation between the art department and the costume designers on all films and especially on productions like *Fiddler on the Roof.* The costume designers submitted their colour schemes to us and we showed them the set colours. In this way the Designer Bob Boyle was able to ensure that he was getting a total harmony of colour on the screen." (*Stringer.*)

Chapter 3
The Designer and the
Production Unit

A great number of factors contributes to the *design* of each image on the cinema screen and each member of the film unit bears some responsibility for one or more aspects of the design content.

The Lighting Cameraman, the Operator and the Designer make their individual contribution and are responsible to the Director for what is recorded by the camera. The Director has to make sure that the action of the story is portrayed convincingly, and he bears the responsibility of ensuring that the overall background into which the action is placed adds to the cinematic illusion. In the best films therefore the Director, the Lighting Cameraman and the Designer work very closely together and they should be of one mind about what is being done. In this way each of them ensures that he will not throw away the value of his colleagues' contributions.

The relationship that the Designer develops with the Director and the Lighting Cameraman is of critical importance in determining whether his role as Designer is going to be truly creative. Some Designers feel at ease with a certain type of Director, perhaps one who will give them a great deal of freedom, or one who insists on building everything in the studio.

A Designer may also have a marked preference for certain types of film just as Directors often work within a particular *genre*.

Ken Adam has a preference for location films and he compares his attitudes to location and studio work:

"As a rule I find location shooting to be much simpler from a designer's point of view than studio shooting where one has to create one's set. In terms of location design one has to have a designer's eye; one has to have taste; and one has to be able to improvise and adapt the locations to the subject matter. In studio films one has to invent everything and make use, particularly in Bond films, of the film craft one has learned—matte shots, models, rear or front projection. This then becomes the test of your know-how in terms of film design as it was originally conceived. In the old days everyone wanted to keep films in studios for a variety of reasons. Studios were so large that it was very convenient to film everything in them. Today, if the subject permits one can make much more use of locations. It is possible to shoot the whole picture on location. The Designer has still an important function. The function is more of concept and of adaptation rather than in technical know-how, in trick work and in creating settings from scratch." (*Adam.*)

In an ideal industry one could imagine the Producer selecting a Director whose record would indicate that he would be suitable for a certain type of script. He might also choose a Designer, perhaps at the recommendation of the Director, who would also derive personal satisfaction from working on that particular script. However, in practice there would seem to be little relationship between the type of script and the Designer selected. The criterion of choice is often of a more arbitrary nature than one based on suitability for the task.

The Designer, therefore, in his assuming responsibility for the art department within a production team is going to have to come to terms with the Director and the Director's own interpretation of a script.

John Stoll expresses it thus:

"All technicians are there to help and serve the Director. If the Designer and the Director disagree about the fundamental interpretation of the script then, of course, there are going to be serious problems. For example, a script may be romantic to the Designer and sordid to the Director. Since the interpretation of the script is going to affect the kind of design one will produce one will have to resolve this apparent conflict at a very early stage." (*Stoll.*)

Some Directors like to exercise a great deal of control over the design content of the film and this may be a result of a possible background in the art department or it may be part of their character to have to control as much as they humanly can within the total production.

"Some directors exercise much greater control over my activities. Michael Relph and Alexander Mackendrick for example are both artists and have very strong ideas about what they want; in fact you are almost working as their assistant because they can be so precise in their visualisations. In these cases each sketch will have to be approved by the Director before being shown to the rest of the department." (*MacGregor.*)

Directors who have a more *literary* than *design* background may leave the design content completely to the Designer.

"Wolf Mankowitz, for example, will be more interested in the dialogue that takes place in one corner of a large set than in using the totality of a set in a dramatic way. Some of the most interesting scenes in *Cleopatra* and especially in *All About Eve* take place in front of two square yards of wallpaper. On the other hand in a film like *2001: A Space Odyssey* one has huge sets and

Battle scene from Cromwell, *a film remarkable for its colour, costumes and historical sets. Designed by John Stoll.*

long stretches of action in which there is no dialogue at all. Not only is there nobody saying anything, there is nobody *to* say anything. Some films are like novels and other films tend to be like paintings." (*Barry.*)

Designers will also find that many contemporary Directors have very fixed ideas about studio shooting or location shooting. There is at present a marked preference for location shooting to add reality to the image. As Tony Richardson remarks elsewhere, "For me studios are death, they are anathema, they are everything I hate." (*Directing Motion Pictures,* published by The Tantivy Press) and this striving for realism may inhibit the use of many effects that have been used in traditional commercial film-making. Michael Stringer illustrates this point in discussing the early stages of planning *Fiddler on the Roof*:

"Norman Jewison wanted an extreme realism because of the subject. This was more of a realistic subject than most large-scale musicals. In every department, such as the camera department for instance, things had to be kept as simple as possible. Helicopter shots were eliminated after discussions between Jewison, Ossie Morris, Bob Boyle and Pat Palmer the Associate Producer. We wanted to get across the simplicity of the story and not go into the *Hello Dolly!* type of format.

"We used no process photography, although we had thought at one stage that we could use front projection for the dawn shots on Tevye's house at the very beginning, but Jewison was very keen to use the location with the real dawn. We went to endless trouble photographing the dawn sky on the location with still photographs at different times of daylight. We arranged the whole set so that we could get the dawn sky behind Tevye's house which would appear in silhouette."

John Stoll makes a similar point in discussing the aversion some directors have towards shots involving models and miniatures:

"Directors are not fond of being tied to a static shot these days and complicated matters involving hanging models are bound to restrict them. Most of the modern Directors do not want back projections or front projections, they want to find a realistic method of achieving the required effect." (*Stoll.*)

The Director most involved with all aspects of his productions is probably Stanley Kubrick. Nothing goes into his films without its passing his scrutiny and he is certainly most actively involved in making design decisions.

"What makes Kubrick's films so interesting is the fact that he has a number of criteria against which he judges everything that goes into the film. He wants to make each single element of the film as interesting as he possibly can by unflagging attention to every detail. Because a film is so complicated with sound, music, photography, acting etc, the sheer quantity of interest one is faced with makes it almost impossible to be bored by anything Kubrick makes." (*Barry.*)

The Art Department

Although initially working alone with the Director, the Designer will have to determine what resources he will need to call upon to help him realise the kind of design necessary for the film. After reading the script through he will have a rough idea of the basic technical problems that he will face, and the Director's own interpretation of the script will have presented other problems, perhaps by insisting on using precise though distant locations, or in wanting to have maximum value from the special effects department.

Whatever the particular situation the Designer will have a great number of technicians and craftsmen to help him in his task. The following is a list of the chief categories of technicians who are at the disposal of the Designer. Obviously, the number chosen will be determined by the budget and the demands of the script.

Highly stylised set by Michael Stringer for Casino Royale.

The Assistant Art Director

He will supervise with the Designer all the working drawings and throughout the production he acts as the Designer's chief assistant.

Chief Draughtsman

He is in charge of all the draughting and obviously is a skilled draughtsman well versed in lenses; laying out; the preparation of drawings; construction; some knowledge of engineering; and decorative detail. He should be able to lay out matte shots and make models.

Draughtsman

He will draw the sets and should be conversant with camera angles and projections, and should have a thorough knowledge of construction, decorative detail, perspective and special effects and should be able to make models.

Junior Draughtsman

Draws full-size details, assists the Draughtsman, helps to make models, and gets the drawings printed in the print room.

Sketch Artist

A Sketch Artist is not always employed—depending very much on the film being made. He works with the Designer in producing continuity sketches and the presentation sketches that the Designer may not have time to do himself. The Sketch Artist often liaises between the Designer and the Director and the Designer and the Draughtsman too, since he must also know how to project a sketch from a plan and elevation. On the other hand he may have to project a rough plan and elevation from a sketch.

Construction Manager

He supervises the construction of the sets and keeps a close eye on the budget, the time sheet, and all the labour. In some films there may be from 50 to 150 craftsmen working for the Designer. The budget is estimated by the Construction Manager and the Cost Accountant with the Designer. They estimate the number of man-days needed during the shooting period and construction period.

Set Dresser

He will help the Designer dress the set. He does research into all the props on the picture even down to the smallest detail, especially if it is a period picture.

Production Buyer

Works with the Designer and Set Dresser. He hires and buys materials and props for the picture. He should know all the main sources of props as well as specialist places that he may need to use, e.g. where one can get reed thatching.

Scenic Artists

The number will depend on the size of the production. They are highly skilled and talented Scene Painters who paint the backings. Backing sizes vary from approximately 10 ft. by 10 ft. to 350 ft. by 36 ft. Cyclorama backings. Scenic Artists touch up or colour photographic Blow-up Backings, Cut-outs and Gauzes, Special Portraits, Murals, Paintings, Glass Paintings and Posters. They paint in any style—maybe several styles in one film. They create period tapestries, oil paintings and literally any graphic work need for the film. Many Scenic Artists have trained in the theatre and they also have a very thorough knowledge of painting media, perspective, period styles and architecture black and white—or photo references, and the Scenic Artist will then enlarge the Backing design and paint the subject on the Backing or Cyclorama. All colours and tones are usually shown to the Lighting Cameraman by the Art Director and Scenic Artist before any work is begun, to make sure that the finished Backing will be correctly lit and photographed.

The Costume Designer

The Costume Designer is of course a very important person in any film unit—whether the film is contemporary, cast in the future or in the past. The co-operation and sharing of ideas between the Costume Designer and Art Director is vital. At every stage of the development of the design the Costume Designer is consulted and kept informed of all the changes in schedule and ideas. After full consultations with the Director and Art Director the Costume

Designer will make colour sketches for further discussion, with fabric samples of every costume.

When casting has been completed, fittings will be made for the cast, and often costume houses like Bermans will be asked to make the costumes especially if the film is a "period" film. Now the cutting and making of the costumes begin, and every stage of this creation will be carefully supervised by the Costume Designer, and when the final fittings have been completed the Director, Producer, Art Director and Costume Designer will scrutinize the costumes most carefully and make definitive adjustments. Often film tests will be made of particular costumes and various samples of fabric will be filmed before a final choice is made. The Lighting Cameraman will also be consulted over colour and texture, and a number of weeks before shooting (depending on the size of the film) the Wardrobe Supervisor will join the unit and take over the costumes, and will be responsible for their maintenance and care during the production.

The Chief Make-up Artist also co-operates most closely with the Art Director and Costume Designer—especially if the film is "'period" or fantasy like *Tales of Beatrix Potter* or *Alice in Wonderland.* The Costume Designer will remain with the film until the last weeks of shooting, and naturally works with the wardrobe staff and the actors and actresses, dealing with all the demands and suggestions and worries that emerge from some performers.

The Costume Designer is a highly skilled artist with a huge knowledge of the history of costume, the cutting of the materials, the enormous range of fabrics, dyes, patterns, fashion, and should be a natural psychologist in working with the actors and actresses.

Carpenters

The Carpenters make the basic flats, rostrums, ceilings, floors and walls of the sets. They make staircases, tables, benches, chairs, and virtually any prop or set piece required. They can make elaborate staircase wreaths, reproduce any period design—and are brilliant craftsmen who can adapt themselves to any of the vast range of requirements which a film demands. Every studio has a carpenters' workshop under the Master Carpenter, and each production has one or more supervisors and chargehands who keep in close contact with the Construction Manager, Art Director and his assistants. A stand-by carpenter is attached to the shooting unit to work with the Unit in striking walls, building camera tracks, and generally helping to make the camera movements smooth and as speedy as possible.

Stagehands

The Stagehands work in moving flats, timber, rostrums, backings from the scene dock or carpenter's shop to the various stages during the preparation or pre-fabrication period, and all through the shooting period of the film. The Stand-by Stagehand works with the Stand-by Carpenter in moving and striking set pieces with the shooting unit.

Plasterers

The Plasterers make the cladding of the sets—brick wall surfaces, stone wall surfaces (thin plaster casts on scrim backings). They make models, moulds and every type of plaster decoration from Egyptian ornaments to Adam Friezes, from granite rock reproductions to oak beams made of fibreglass or vacuum formed plastic. They work with a variety of materials: plaster, clay, fibreglass, vacuum formed plastics, polyeurathene, polyzote, concrete, foam rubber, latex, "Vinamould" and vermiculite. Columns, pilasters, statues, mouldings, crests, swags, are all made by the Plasterers under the supervision of the Master Plasterer. The Plasterers' workshop accumulates a vast stock of all these items, and the versatility of the Plasterers is enormous.

Modellers

Modellers work closely with the Art Director in making special modelled props or set pieces—like some special statue for the film or a series of fantasy trees. They make scale model maquettes of certain pieces—so that the scale model can be referred to in the actual building period. They model decorative ornaments in clay or plastecine and are highly skilled artists—again with great knowledge of ornament, sculpture and methods of construction.

Painters

Once the set has been built by the Carpenters, clad by the Plasterers and set on the stage or pre-fab area the Painters take over and finish the set with their brushes and spray guns. The Painters under the Master Painter are adept at producing any texture, colour and tone asked for by the Art Director. They produce wall textures with a wide variety of paint materials and if for instance a wall should look very old and decayed they will coat the surface with thick impasto "'surfex"—and continue to paint, sandpaper, wax and scrape the surface until the final texture looks exactly like the real wall—perhaps one hundred years old. They "age" sets by "dusting" with spray guns, waxing with rags soaked in white spirit and powder paint and wax. They will crackle the paint surface, coat it with various varnishes, run "dirty" water over it and perhaps burn off areas with a blowgun. They may be called upon to prepare ballroom floors with elaborate geometric patterns, and highly polished surfaces which will mean silk screening hundreds of square yards of highly complex patterns and then carefully laying it on strong paper backings on hessian. Often they will make marble paper for panels or columns and perhaps a specially designed wallpaper which may be unobtainable from a wallpaper manufacturer. The Painters also paint backings or cyclorama backings perhaps thirty-six feet high by three hundred feet long. Attached to the paintshop is the *Signwriters* workshop. The Signwriters are accomplished in painting, silk-screening and stencils, lettering, and signwriting of every possible description from the smallest reproduction letterheading or illuminated page, from a medieval manuscript to a poster one hundred feet long. They can silkscreen any pattern needed, and make appliqué crests, posters and pub signs.

Riggers

The Riggers erect the tubular scaffolding on which many sets are braced and supported, especially exterior sets on the studio lot or on location. When heavy set walls have to be mobile ("floaters") the walls will be clipped to tubular frames on heavy duty wheels for easy floating (or moving). The Riggers also hang the lighting spotrails, and build tubular mobile lighting towers on wheels from ten feet high to thirty feet high. They might be called upon to build camera towers as high as eighty feet or more. They also erect rostrums on wheels for the Painters and Scenic Artists—for example in order

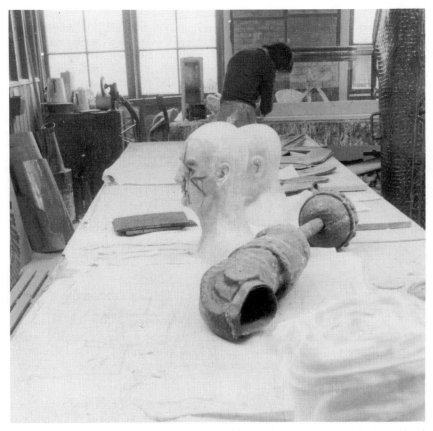

A view of the plaster shop at M-G-M/EMI Studios, Boreham Wood, England.

to paint a cyclorama backing, tubular towers thirty-six inches high will be built, with levels every ten feet for the Painters and Scenic Artists to work upon. They will also build rostrum floor areas—sometimes of considerable size—three hundred feet by one hundred and fifty feet by six feet high.

Drapery Department
"The Drapes" are upholsterers who sew up the backings—floors, and often sew up scenic canvas backings three hundred feet by thirty-six feet (and gauzes of the same size) and help to erect the gauzes. They make all the curtains, upholster chairs and sofas, make table-cloths, cushions and anything in fabric. The department holds a large collection of stock curtains and fabrics, and they work with many varieties of material from velvet to grass matting, and are—as with all departments in a film studio—extremely efficient and versatile.

Property Department

The Property Master supervises the proproom which houses the studio stock and the incoming hired or purchased "props." The property men "dress" the sets with the hired furniture—and they work closely with the Art Director, Set Dresser, and Property Buyer in placing each piece of furniture or prop in its place on the set. If the set is a garden the property men will arrange the flowers, bushes and artificial grass—if it is not "real." If the grass or trees are living then Studio Gardeners will dress the set. The shooting unit usually has a chargehand property man "stand-by" with one or two property men, who work with the unit in moving the furniture or dressings on the set—keeping all the continuity props carefully, and anticipating every move on the set. On a location a Property Master has his own prop truck—well equipped with a vast array of "hand" props (like spectacles, watches, walking sticks, umbrellas etc.) and all his equipment for digging, brushing, watering, cutting and prop-making. The Property Master knows the script by heart and can make sure that all the vital props are always at hand and on the set in the shortest possible time. The Set Dresser, Property Master, Property Dressers and Property Buyer work as a team, and are always in very close contact with the Art Director, Director and Assistant Director.

Property Makers

Often small, intimate props are required and, because of the special nature of these props, they often have to be specially made. Property Makers make up things like old parchment scrolls, a watch with an unusual dial, a milk churn, an oversized giant leaf, a hundred exotic artificial plants. They will make props in conjunction with all the departments in a film studio, or on location in conjunction with local craftsmen and local materials.

Metal Workers

Metal Workers are skilled in shaping metal to any shape or size and often work in conjunction with the Special Effects department. Metal Workers will construct metal armatures or frames for sculptural pieces, for artificial trees or topiary work. They will make spiral staircases, spaceship frames, special seats for an actor to sit upon with perhaps a revolving or swaying motion. They may be called upon to make the framework for a submarine or aircraft interior, or a zeppelin or rocket. They make multiple pom-pom guns, spears, swords, shields, and work in every type of metal, aluminium, iron, steel or brass and copper. They will make water-tanks for underwater shooting, monorails, dummy tanks, railway engines, and rostrums on gimbels for rocking cars, aircraft, coaches.

Special Effects

Generally this section comprises two departments, the Physical Special Effects and the Photographic Effects. The Physical Special Effects cater for effects such as smoke, mist, rain, fire, wind and explosions. They have equipment for making all these natural effects and lay out their various machines to the requirements of the Director and Art Director. They will organise under the head of their department the aero engine wind machines to produce a snow blizzard using either polyeurathene or polyzote capsules, or marble dust. They will "rain in" a complete street or square on the lot or stage or location with rain machines—or produce a moving, motorised camera track for shooting a miniature spaceship or aircraft. Miniature ships, aircraft, cars, tanks and even people will be activated by special effects.

On a war film all the explosions, gas operated machine guns, flame throwers, fires and collapsing houses or exploding aircraft will be operated by the Special Effects team.

The Photographic Effects produce the matte paintings, the inserted moving plates in a miniature space ship or building. This department will produce animated frame by frame inserts into any part of the frame area. Matte artists paint the areas of picture on glass (or other materials) above or below "the matte line"—(see visual examples). They often work in oil paints and are extremely skilful artists who can paint realistically and produce paintings which will, when re-photographed, look exactly like a photograph. Peter Ellenshaw, Albert Whitlock and Alen Maley work in America on matte paintings, and have perfected the technique by not painting "too tightly"—their style is loose and fairly free, and consequently their paintings photograph very realistically. In England matte artists like Ray Capel, Cliff Culley, Gerald Larne, Ivor Beddoes, Les Bowie, Peter Woods and Peter Melrose all paint matte paintings in the same way, and their results are uniformly excellent. Unfortunately this subject is too vast to cover fully in the scope of this book, and it is only possible to draw the reader's attention to the fact that this facet of film-making is extremely important and valuable.

Even after the budget has been determined a check has to be kept on the progress of the construction on a day to day basis. The Construction Manager is an invaluable help to the Designer throughout the shooting period since at any one time he will know how many carpenters, painters etc, he will need. Although one can project requirements, needs fluctuate. One may need fifty men at the beginning of construction and after a few weeks one may require but a dozen. The Construction Manager is always in a position to note the progress of building and when men can be laid off.

Budget

The Art Department budget is nowadays subject to a great number of variable factors and it is no longer possible to find a direct relation between this budget and the total budget of the film.

"The cost of the set construction used to be about ten per cent of the total budget of the film but now there is a great deal of variance. Nor can one be dogmatic about what kind of films are the cheapest to design. Location films could be reasonably inexpensive if all the locations are in existence and need no re-building; on the other hand on a location film one has the expense of transportation of equipment and personnel and on a big film the expenses in this area can be enormous." (*Stringer.*)

Perhaps the only reasonable generalisation that can be made in view of the wide variety of scripts is that shooting in a controlled environment close to the main centre of operations is probably going to be cheaper than taking a unit a vast distance on location. A good efficient crew, including a good Designer, can make excellent sets within a very small space if necessary. Some Directors of course object to a studio environment and that is their privilege but (given the inevitable shortage of money) indulging the Director's whim can sometimes prove disastrously expensive.

Organising Work

The Designer is responsible for organising the work of everyone in the Art Department. Economy of production can only be achieved if the Designer knows at each stage in the preparation of the film what he himself should be doing and what the others in the Art Department should be doing. At all stages in the shooting period he should know what is going to be shot in the subsequent few days.

"It is terribly important to be well organised—I hate working in a muddle. Of course there are many ways of organising a film but one should know what one is aiming at. For me setting the film out in detail clarifies things and makes life a lot easier. I write down what work is to be done while other work is being done. I know exactly what amount of work has to be done for future shots. Some directors do not like this sort of thing. The older directors usually like it but some of the younger ones will think that you are trying to do their job, but it isn't that at all. Planning is a great help when you need economical production. If you come up with a sketch of the bow of a submarine and the Director says that is exactly what he wants, you would not have to build a whole submarine for that shot. If you haven't quite made up your mind about the shot beforehand you cannot afford to take a chance and you may have to build a whole submarine for the one shot. It's like building a set with four walls and a roof in a studio. I may be old-fashioned but I still believe much of film-making is to do with the business of creating illusions." (*Cain.*)

Schedule

To help him with his planning the Designer will produce a Schedule or progress chart. This can be a very complicated affair which will summarise the progress on each set for the duration of his involvement with the film. It will probably note the responsibilities of those working in the Art Department and will certainly give at-a-glance deadlines for all construction.

Each Designer has his own method of devising his schedule. As an example of one Designer's method Syd Cain describes how he approaches the organisation of shooting on location:

"After breaking down the script into phases and sets we then work out how many days shooting we will need. This is the Production Manager's job but I work my own timetable out as well. The value of this is that at a glance I can see that we have six and a half days in one place and another three and a half days close by; giving ten days in one area. One should try to keep travel to a minimum and arrange one's schedule taking this factor into account. It is best to keep the unit for two weeks in one area if possible since this gives me time to prepare for the next move. A lot of moving about does not help the Art Department because I will have to have two units on the go. One would be with the shooting unit, the other travelling in advance preparing the locations." (*Cain.*)

Preparing the Budget

It behoves all members of the production unit who are in a position to spend production funds to spend them wisely. The Design Department no less than any other department is capable of absorbing vast sums. Some expenses can be clearly forecast, others are more difficult to anticipate or

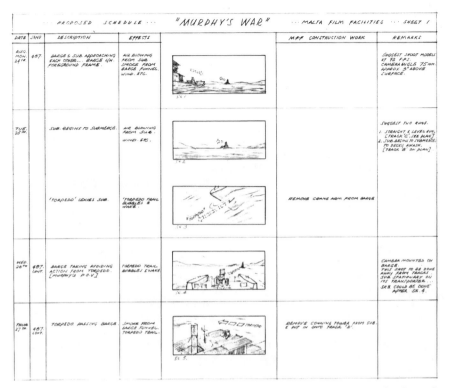

An example of thorough planning. Murphy's War. *Designer (not credited) Syd Cain.*

avoid. The Designer will make his initial budget assessments during his first readings of the script.

"The most important thing to learn is how to break down the story and translate it to the screen in the most economical way possible. You have to remember that you are involved in a business. The Designer has to submit a budget. He has to estimate what he thinks the film will cost. The company already has its own idea of a budget because it has an accountant who has to do an overall pilot budget and in that pilot budget so much is allowed for the Art Department. The Designer puts in one figure and the accountant his. The accountant's figure is invariably lower. Between the two, a realistic budget is worked out. This I find the hardest part of the Designer's job. There are basically three ways of doing it. We will discount one way immediately since that depends on experience and one cannot *learn* experience (I can now pick up a script and after reading it say roughly how much it will cost). Another method is to break down the script into sets and estimate roughly how much each set is going to cost and then total up and add ten per cent. Again, experience is important because one can look at a set and give a rough figure, say £8,000. A third method is based on estimated shooting time. You may be told that it is going to be an eight week picture—that is eight weeks on the floor. The most one can spend in a week of building is £4,000. On this basis an eight week film will cost about £32,000. This is very rough estimate of labour and materials. On top of this are the props. (Costumes are a different department altogether.)" (*Cain.*)

Ken Adam explains his approach to budgeting the Bond films:

"Now that I have done a number of Bond films we have a vague idea of how much it will cost before we start—we are not more than ten per cent out one way or another. I find the most successful way of budgeting from the point of view of art direction is to calculate the labour force you need to put up your set. One would then have a figure of X number of men for Y number of weeks. To this cost add roughly sixty per cent for materials and this is one's budget." (*Adam.*)

After arriving at a rough figure the Designer will know if the amount allotted to the Art Department by the Producer will be insufficient or adequate. At this stage the Designer will have to go through each scene in the script very carefully indeed, probably with the Construction Manager to determine the cost of each set that has been proposed. Often a few lines in the script will involve big expense and the Designer may have to recommend changes in the action.

"Just a couple of lines could involve a tremendous amount of building and money and we would either cut the scene out altogether or cut it down. We might examine one piece of action in the story and ask if it is really necessary to the development of the story. It may not add anything to the whole but it may prove expensive in time and building." (*Cain.*)

Chapter 4
Designing Locations

The Script and Location Shooting
The script is the starting point in the Designer's search for suitable locations. When considering the script the Designer has to get a broad understanding of the type of action involved and relate this to the kind of location that would be required.

"Although one may go out and find an ideal location for a film, unless the story is believable the film will fail regardless of the excellence of the locations. It is the story that is the most important factor. If it is a romantic story then the sets should be treated romantically or beautifully. In the film *Greengage Summer* I used classical French sets as a background for an English school girl's romantic vision of France—they were basically an expression of her dream world. This atmosphere was created by the script and it is always the script that should create the atmosphere." (*Stoll.*)

After reading through the script the Designer will have an impression of the kind of location he will need but inevitably this initial visualisation will have to be modified. One rarely finds locations that are exactly like the original visualisation. Having selected a particular location, it will become the starting point for the action and a new set of visualisations. John Stoll observes:

"One always finds something other than what one is looking for and it is from what one finds that the picture begins to emerge. There is no location that is completely acceptable to the story: one may have to shoot in Spain when the story takes place in Algeria etc. One has to re-interpret the script and of course, this is what design is all about."

Finding Locations
Before deciding which location is suitable for one or more pieces of action one will have to research the location thoroughly and probably examine many other possibilities too.

In adapting *Macbeth* for the screen problems arose in relating the requirements of Shakespeare's action to actual Scottish castles.

"I saw these castles in Scotland and I am quite sure that Shakespeare had never been to Scotland because the design of Scottish castles is quite incompatible with the design requirements of the play. In fact Dunsinane castle bore no relationship to the story. Not one of the original castles was suitable for the film for a variety of reasons and I don't see how they ever could have been even at the time of Shakespeare. Scottish castles are very different from English castles, being more like fortified houses. English castles are built around a centre keep." (*Shingleton.*)

Extensive photographic research can be an essential part of the selection of difficult locations.

"We then started looking at those locations which had interested us most. In some cases, for example the interior of a flat, we had an overwhelming choice and we photographed the interiors of several hundred flats.

"Kubrick examined the photographs and selected some that seemed, at least in part, suitable for the film. We never did find a flat that was completely suitable including its dressing, which was a pity because it might have had that lovely lived-in sort of look." (*Barry.*)

When searching for a suitable location for the exterior shots of Alex's house in *A Clockwork Orange* Jonathan Barry and Stanley Kubrick considered very wide ranging possibilities:

"The exterior was shot at Thamesmead, one of the most advanced residential developments in the world. At one stage we had considered using the Habitat site in Montreal and we had also considered the flats at the Barbican development in London but these were only half completed at the time of shooting. The Barbican flats also tend to be rather tall and out of the picture and would not have given us the effect we were after." (*Barry.*)

In the search for a suitable location the Designer should always be concerned with the practical problems presented by the location and whether the location looks right from the point of view of the narrative:

"The Designer should be able to help the Director in his choice of location. For example what may be perfect in every other way may be devoid of sunshine at a crucial time of day because it lies in the shadow of other buildings or perhaps it might face north instead of south. Some locations may be permanently covered in mist and it might seem common sense to avoid these places but it is surprising how many times disastrous mistakes have been made through lack of foresight and consultation with all concerned." (*Stringer.*)

"Looking for locations can be very boring. On *Where Eagles Dare* we drove from castle to castle each being three or four hours' drive from the rest over a period of several weeks." (*Mullins.*)

Preparing a location set for On Her Majesty's Secret Service. *Designed by Syd Cain.*

James Bond films have also relied on spectacular locations and none was perhaps more exceptional than Blofeld's headquarters in *O.H.M.S.S.*

"When working on the film *O.H.M.S.S.*, we searched all over Europe for the right location. We needed a place for Blofeld to have his headquarters and quite by luck we went to Switzerland and stumbled upon a building at eleven thousand feet. The owners were in the process of building a restaurant and club. We wanted to build according to our specifications and we were given permission to do so on condition that we made it into a permanent structure." (*Cain.*)

Wilfrid Shingleton tells of his search for suitable castles for *Macbeth*:

"When it came to looking for castle locations we found that those that hadn't been ruined by re-designing over the centuries were in such a dilapidated condition that one could do little with them. We also found that any castle that was in good condition was usually in a town and quite impossible to shoot. Polanski, who had already shot *Cul-de-Sac* on Lindisfarne decided that Bamburgh and Lindisfarne might be the best castles to use. Lindisfarne was the smaller castle of the two and after making a more interesting silhouette by building on, it was quite suitable for Macbeth's castle. Bamburgh Castle (which was close to Lindisfarne and therefore convenient from the point of view of scheduling) would work for the much bigger Dunsinane Castle." (*Shingleton.*)

Location Recce

Having read through the script and decided on a few possible districts in which to search for suitable locations the Designer will spend some time travelling around with, possibly, the Director and the Producer, along with the Production Manager. There is no fixed rule about who does the recce but the Director and the Production Manager will have their own contributions to make to the decisions. The Designer should equip himself with his tools of location research:

A large scale map of the district with mileage radii drawn from the main communications centre.

A camera with which he can take as many photographs as necessary including "panning" photographs covering up to 360° coverage, in black-and-white and colour film.

Meter Stick.

Ruler and Tape Measure.

Compass.

Guide book to the district.

Sketch Book.

As many postcards of the district as are available and relevant should be purchased.

If the location is made up of buildings etc, one should make a detailed note of any structural changes that have to be made, or occupants who have to be evacuated for the period of the shooting. Buildings that may be used should be thoroughly photographed with measurements taken. If alterations have to be made each job has to be accurately budgeted and a total budget for the entire location to be added to the budget of other locations. It may happen that the alterations necessary to buildings will not be warranted by the importance of that sequence to the script, making script excisions necessary.

The topography of the site should be noted especially in relation to the rising and setting of the sun:

"When one chooses a location one should always take into account the position of the sun—where it rises and where it sets. In *Fiddler* we had some marvellous sunset shots from the synagogue which was deliberately placed in relation to the sun's setting position.

"When one has to build extra sets on location one has to build on a site where the sun positions can be calculated to suit the dramatic needs of that location. For this reason one should always go around with a compass and the largest scale maps that one can find." (*Stringer.*)

If the location includes tidal water, the high and low water levels should be taken note of to ensure that disasters do not occur. At least one film has been held up by the water level of a river rising sufficiently to flood the location that had been built—when accidents like this occur the blame is rightly attributed to the Designer for not doing his homework.

Clever adaptation of an existing disused sugar mill for Macho Callahan. *Designed by Ted Marshall.*

(*Above*) *Turkish house used for some interior shots in* Charge of the Light Brigade. *Designed by Ted Marshall.* (*Below*) *Dramatic use of an unusual sand dune location in* Lawrence of Arabia. *Designed by John Box.*

Weather statistics should also be consulted especially if one wishes to use natural weather conditions. If one has to resort to artificial snow or artificial weather in general, then the extra expense must be included in the budget.

Exceptional weather conditions may have to be allowed for when shooting in extreme climates as in the desert or on mountain peaks. Discussing early problems met with in *O.H.M.S.S.*, Syd Cain remarks:

"The building had to stand a wind of 120 miles an hour. Our engineers were quite used to these problems—they had recently been working on the Simplon tunnel. Working in such a situation you will get many headaches apart from the purely design problems. The weather was one factor. The location was ideal for us because it would have been impossible to reproduce this kind of vista in a studio. Oddly enough, it was so perfect that sometimes it didn't look real and to give it more natural feeling we encouraged some birds to fly past the windows." (*Cain.*)

Weather Cover Sets and Temporary Studios

If indoor shooting has to take place on location then a careful 'check should be made on any building that could make suitable indoor shooting space. It makes obvious sense for the chosen building to be situated close to the outdoor location so that in the event of inclement weather the schedule can be arranged to shoot indoors. If one's indoor location is at too great a distance then bad weather can easily mean one or more days' shooting lost. The places to look for are:

Existing prefabricated buildings.

Farms.

Factories.

Warehouses.

Garages.

Large old houses.

Partial ruins.

Actual interiors of houses or offices.

Covered streets (particularly in European locations).

Flats can easily be constructed to transform the interior of a location building if the actual interior is unsuitable. This procedure was adopted in the filming of Lindsay Anderson's film *O Lucky Man*, part of which is shot in a disused school building. Some of the interiors of *A Clockwork Orange* were shot in a location factory, and there are other examples.

Permissions

Written permission to shoot on a location should always be given before the production company proceeds with a location that seems suitable. The local municipal authority is normally approached if one wishes to shoot in a public area, but in the case of using private property the legal owner has to be approached and an arrangement will have to be negotiated. Letters of permission will originate at the production office and are the responsibility of the Production Manager—hence the desirability of having the Production Manager with the Designer and the Director on location recces.

Local Contacts

When shooting on location one should always start by finding local contacts. Some countries are so eager to gain foreign currencies that the government will supply the film production company with a great deal of help. Syd Cain describes the setting up of location shooting in Yugoslavia.

"When shooting location work one always starts with local contacts. If we take the case of *The Iron Daffodil*, we looked all over Europe for a good place to film and eventually decided on Yugoslavia. In Yugoslavia there is a government department that deals with foreign film companies and having heard our requirements they will initiate a search for a suitable location. They have the script and a list of requirements sent to them by the producers. They then look around and get any necessary permissions. When they have completed this first stage, they then send for me to have a look at the locations they have found. (This procedure is not common. One usually finds a location first and then gets permission afterwards.) Of course what they find may not be suitable and one has to start looking around once more. If it is necessary to use a real Yugoslav village in a film, the government will send all the villagers on holiday while we re-build or add to the village. Another factor at play in this film is that the village must look French. This would tie the location down to northern Yugoslavia where because the villages do look quite French, having red tiled roofs, white walls and window shutters, we would not have to do much conversion." (*Cain.*)

The Yugoslavian government department that deals with foreign film production companies supplied a location manager for *Fiddler on the Roof*.

"The Yugoslav location manager was very helpful indeed in suggesting locations and Bob Boyle and I, along with Norman Jewison and the production team, covered every village and every single place within a thirty mile radius of our chosen main location." (*Stringer.*)

Local contacts are essential when negotiating with landowners and property owners. One entire location may be spread across the land of a whole village and to obtain permission to shoot and otherwise tamper with the land separate permissions have to be obtained from each individual owner. Ted Marshall had this problem in *The Charge of the Light Brigade*.

"The military advisor to the film came across an excellent location by accident while driving around in a jeep. He was very excited by what he saw but on inquiry we found that this valley was divided into eight separate villages." (*Marshall.*)

In *The Last Valley* the problem was greater because the land was divided into very small plots.

"The village was spread over about three or four acres and sixty farmers owned land on that acreage. The actual contact with owners is the Production Manager's job. You have to be very careful how you handle people—especially when you want to do something on their land. Once you have stated what you want it is the responsibility of the production department to negotiate with the farmer on whose land you are working." (*Mullins.*)

Location interior sketch of old cottage by Ted Marshall for Charlie Bubbles.

Location Interiors

For reasons of economy or authenticity it may be decided to shoot a film either partially or totally using location interiors. The first practical problem to be dealt with is finding a suitable location interior in which to shoot. This can be a time consuming process, for while in the studio one can build precisely what one needs, using a location inevitably means making some compromises in one's conception.

One must evaluate how much re-building will be necessary; how much re-painting will be necessary; and how much dressing will have to be found. If the location is a house then one will have to consider the occupants—will they be offered alternative accommodation. Tenants or owners of suitable property also have to be approached in the first instance with regard to permission to shoot in the location and this initial approach has to be tactful, and one should be willing to conform to any conditions that have been attached to the agreement once an agreement has been signed. Re-building or painting has to be done with the owner's consent and normally one will have to leave the location in its original state after the film has been completed.

Analysis of the Location Interior Set

When the most suitable location has been found it should be carefully analysed before any transformation is proceeded with. The following points to note are intended as a guide only. Every room has its own peculiarities and every script its own specific requirements. The Designer will have the requirements of the script in mind when making his analysis.

Walls:
plain or textured?
wall paper, well-worn or clean?

Cornice and Frieze:
patterned or plain?

Woodwork:
waxed or blown down?

Floor:
boarded or carpeted?

Window:
day or night?
blinds?
curtains?
nets?
lace?

Light fittings:
chandelier or gas light?
table lamp etc?

Props:
table or chairs?
made in studio or readymades?

History of the room:
owned by whom?
built when?
rented?
etc.

Character of the room.

Selection of the best angles in the room.

Forced perspective or not?

Ted Marshall describes the preparation of a cottage used in the film *Charlie Bubbles*.

"We shot the cottage scenes in an actual location cottage in Eadale, Derbyshire. We used a few of the rooms but the owner of the cottage was living there the whole time so there was no question of us being able to do any structural alterations or even make any major changes to the house. We re-painted some of the house and made minor alterations to detail in the decoration that seemed to fit in with the character of the film story. For example, we put a few decorative tiles near the window in the kitchen because we felt that the woman in the story would bring some of the city culture to her country cottage when she moved in. She was after all an exile from London who moves to the country after the breakdown of her marriage. We didn't do a finished job with the tiles because we felt that she would most likely start the job herself and leave the work unfinished—she didn't have a man about the house and in her state of mind would most likely not have the motivation to finish jobs that take a concerted effort over a period of time. Curtain materials were also changed to bring out this feeling of an intrusive suburban culture." (*Marshall.*)

In *A Clockwork Orange* two principal location interiors were used. The author's house and the "cat lady's" house were both occupied residences and needed to be thoroughly re-dressed. The amount of available dressing reflected Kubrick's love of having a multitude of options from which to choose. Some modifications to the interiors were also necessary.

"We modified the location interior by getting rid of a number of windows. The exterior was another location and we ran into difficulty making the two locations work with each other. It was difficult to get the movement from the door to the living room to work and I built a hall in the canteen tent in the garden.

"The door of the house in which we were shooting came straight in towards the camera set-up. The door of the exterior location house worked in a different way and it was quite clearly not the same house—the door opening into a very different interior. I put a wooden wall at the end of the room and did the same thing on the other house." (*Barry.*)

Location interiors can also be modified by building sets within the interior. One may for example find a disused school or factory premise into which one can fit a number of small sets. This procedure has been adopted in the filming of *O Lucky Man.* Alan Withy has designed sets that fit into the classrooms and assembly hall of a large disused private school building in Barons Court, London. This kind of conversion job needs a first-class draughtsman and carpenter team but since the rental on such a building will probably be relatively low and since the production unit can hire its own labour force rather than hiring the labour of a large studio at inflated studio prices, the economy of converting existing locations can be worthwhile.

The biggest practical problem in placing built sets in a converted premises is the danger of building too small for the comfort of the camera crew.

"If one uses location interiors with built sets one has to make sure that one leaves enough elbow room for shooting. There is no economy in building location sets that need to be further modified to enable the camera to be put in place." (*Stringer.*)

If there is a normal use of a large building concurrent with shooting then scheduling may become a problem.

"The bathroom had to be specially built in one of the production offices. We took over a factory for a number of the sets and it proved very convenient. The café was built there to make scheduling easier. Scheduling can be a problem when using locations which are in constant use by other people. Changing one's schedule can lead to all kinds of difficulties." (*Barry.*)

Matching location exteriors (above) with studio interiors (opposite) calls for great attention to lighting and design detail. Taste the Blood of Dracula. *Designer Scott MacGregor.*

Dressing Restricted Sets

Although location interior sets need not be small they very often are, even if there is no use of a built set. The camera angle and the lens therefore become important in that they can make the small set seem bigger. Although normal procedure is to dress the set without reference to the camera viewfinder until the shot is almost ready to be taken, much more use of the viewfinder is necessary when shooting in a restricted space.

"Designing for small areas can make things easier in many ways. In location interiors one will often shoot with a wide-angle lens which will prevent the director from moving the camera about to any great extent because of distortion problems. Also, because of the cramped space the designer is going to be concerned with only a few viewpoints. Because of these factors the actual shots taken will have more screen time than they might if the same action is planned for studio shooting where with a greater choice of lens the director will have more freedom of movement. With the camera limited to a single position one can almost dress the set to the camera. In the studio one dresses everything and hopes things will be shown in the right relationship on the screen. In restricted spaces one can dress much more carefully and to one specific angle. Having watched the action one can look through the lens and place things very carefully, sometimes moving things around to get the best composition. On these occasions one has to work very closely with the camera operator. If he is good then one can achieve a great deal." (*Marshall.*)

Much of *A Clockwork Orange* was shot in location interiors using wide angle lenses:

"In the café location he [Kubrick] shot with very wide-angle lenses and this is one of the reasons why the film was shot in academy ratio—we had a much greater range of lenses. When using wide-angle lenses one has to be careful how one moves the camera because of the distortion factor. Luckily the operator was very good and did some excellent hand-held tracking shots." (*Barry.*)

Studio Reconstruction of Location Exteriors

There are occasions when it is necessary to reproduce a location exterior in the studio. It is often an expensive undertaking especially if it is not the way in which the shooting has been planned. The success of the building will depend on the accuracy of one's observation of the location and there is a great deal of painstaking recording to be done.

"I had to co-ordinate the set building back at Pinewood where we shot the interior sequences. We re-built Tevye's farmyard for all the dance numbers at night. We discussed various ways of shooting it on location but because of the dangers of rain, storms, and considerable lighting problems, we thought it better to re-build on the stage at Pinewood with night backings. The realism in fact did not suffer. Of course a re-building job like this meant that we had to find old timbers to match the ones we had found in Yugoslavia. We had covered everything well with stills and measured drawings. Even the minutest detail was recorded." (*Stringer.*)

"One can get away with quite a lot since the audence tends to forget what is *outside* once they have been taken *inside*. I always try to start with an absolutely accurate plan of the whole house. This gives me a clear picture of the relationship between the various rooms even though we may not use all of them in the film. We had the same problem on *The Pumpkin Eater*. The front of the house in St. Peter's Square was very recognisable and we reproduced it in the studio. We then enlarged the rooms at the back of the house to make shooting easier. Somebody who lived in the square remarked to me that he didn't know that any of the houses there were as big as the one we had used. The total effect was so convincing." (*Marshall.*)

Matching Location Exterior with Studio Interior

Location exteriors are often used to give greater reality to a scene which is mainly shot within the studio. The exterior of a large house can set the mood and say a great deal about the occupants, although the shot may be used only briefly in the film. To build the house within the studio would prove to be expensive and it is much easier to find an actual house that fits into the script and then rely on matching the exterior shots with studio shots of the interior.

Quite obviously the interior built in the studio has to be convincing not only as an interior but as the interior to a very particular *exterior*. If possible one should photograph and measure the interior of the location house so that one can re-create as far as possible the location interior in the studio, rather than working from a purely imaginative base. The entrances will create most practical problems since one may be looking out into a garden etc, which will also be shot on location.

"We used a location mansion in *Life at the Top*. The arrangement of the rooms was re-constructed in the studio. We took a few shots inside the bedroom but mostly we used the studio re-constructions. The garden was also re-built in the studio. We used a location house because of its atmosphere. An important part of the action was a large garden party with a lot of movement between the exterior and the ground floor interior. We needed, therefore, a great deal of location material to provide the right feeling for the house as a whole. We couldn't have done this in the studio—at least not in the same way and probably with inferior results. I did that sort of thing in the past—one would devote an entire stage to the exterior of a house and a garden. The whole thing would take about six weeks to build. We also needed a modern house for Laurence Harvey and Jean Simmons. Again we used a location exterior which we used for approach and entry shots. The rest of the house was built in the studio. The great problem of course is in matching location exteriors to studio interiors and being convincing." (*Marshall.*)

Matching Studio Interior with Studio Exterior

Similar problems arise when working completely in the studio. The basic principle to work from is not to allow the interior to be completely cut off from the exterior. The character of the street or whatever the exterior setting happens to be should be allowed to overlap into the interior. Jack Shampan describes how he has matched exterior with interior locations in a film in preparation:

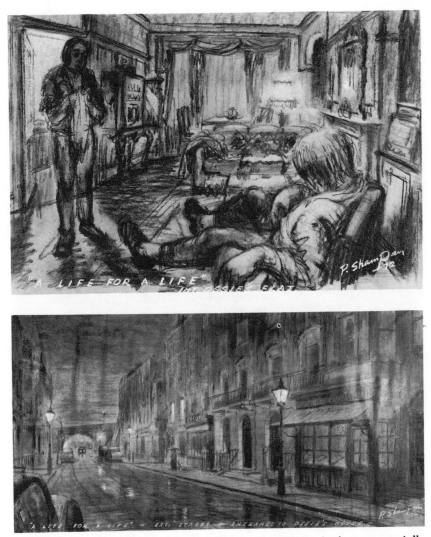

Life for a Life *interior and matching exterior. Designer Jack Shampan carefully matches both locations to ensure continuity of mood after the characters enter the house.*

9am. Sabado. Dec: 6th 1969.

Delightfully atmospheric sketch by Ted Marshall for Macho Callahan.

"We tie up the action as the men enter the house so that the exterior and the interior match—in this instance we're helped because it is a night shot. We can use street lamp illumination that is visible through the window as a link between interior and exterior. One has to find something of this nature which can be common to both interior and exterior. In this set-up we use a scenic backing that is discernible through the window and we will use a street lamp that can be seen just outside the window in the foreground of the exterior." (*Shampan.*)

Matching Dressing
Dressing should be carefully matched when there is a studio reconstruction of a location interior:

"When dressing a location interior we use drapes etc., that we know we will take back with us to the studio. In the studio it is much easier to have net curtains over windows if one has painted backgrounds. In *Life at the Top* I put net curtains over the windows in the studio and when we went on location everyone said that they didn't like the net curtains—so I took them down. But when we returned to the studio I had to put them up again to soften the background which was a painted backing. Somehow no one seemed to notice." (*Marshall.*)

Chapter 5
Preparing Locations

John Stoll has already remarked that locations are seldom everything that one needs and one should be prepared to work hard to change the character of the location as found, to that of the story. The changes involved may be no more than a few alterations to the exterior of a building to change its period or colour. Often, however, one may have to alter an entire landscape by either ploughing or planting. Ted Marshall had to transform a whole valley to make it suitable for shooting *Charge of the Light Brigade.*

"The valley had to be drained because there was too much green. The green had to be ploughed up and teams of tractors spent day after day getting rid of all evidence that the valley had been under agriculture. We hadn't to do anything with the soil colour since after being ploughed and levelled the valley had the colour of a desert. Of course we did have problems when it rained. The surface changed to thin mud for the top inch or two. It was a big problem during the first two weeks of shooting in the camp. After some heavy rain it turned into a quagmire." (*Marshall.*)

A valley that is heavily cultivated is obviously going to cost more to use, and in using cultivated land one has to be prepared to provide for the livelihood of the farmers as well as return the land to its original state at the termination of shooting.

"In *The Last Valley* we did the whole film on location. We had only two

The Last Valley *Complete reconstruction of a Mediaeval village in life size. Great use of museum material was made to ensure complete accuracy of detail. Opposite, the village after a real snowfall. Designed by Peter Mullins.*

weeks out of seventeen in the studio and we ran into bad weather. We built whole villages—a complete church and burgomasters' house-barns; all kinds of things complete with interiors. The idea was to shoot both inside and out on location. We took a valley that was suitable after I had travelled extensively in Italy and Switzerland. It had to have no power cables, pylons etc. It had a couple of houses that we had to re-build and we screened off another group of houses using forty foot trees. We bought up all the crops for the next six months and then had to re-farm the land. It was our intention to re-create the original strip culture instead of having one vast area under crop. The village was built and everything made to appear very authentic. It took four months to finish the job." (*Mullins.*)

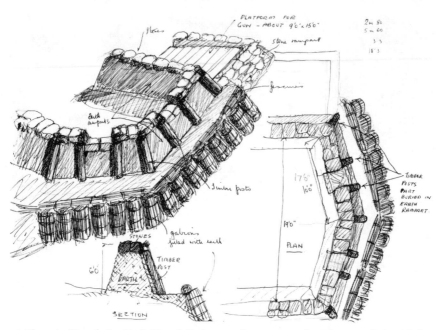

(*Above*) *Sketch by Ted Marshall for earth ramparts in* Charge of the Light Brigade. (*Opposite*) *Ramparts as seen in the film.*

Drawings and photographs play an extensive role in transforming locations that need re-modelling. The Designer can work from photographs of the actual location and draw on to the photograph the changes that he wants to make. These changes should be extremely detailed so that the technicians will know exactly what they have to do. Every part of a location that will appear on screen has to be analysed to ensure there will be nothing incongruous appearing in shot. Pylons and telegraph poles have become such an essential part of the contemporary landscape that it is sometimes easy to forget they are present. Likewise, other signs of contemporary culture such as, for example, radio aerials attached to buildings can easily be overlooked.

Complete drawings of the location *before* and *after* alterations should be produced for the benefit of the whole unit.

Multiple Locations

Sometimes a script may require that a number of villages should feature in the action, each separated by a few or more miles. From the scheduling point of view this would cause great difficulty and in any case finding perhaps six similar locations would be unwarranted in time and expense.

One simple answer to the problem is to use six different parts of one

village, giving the screen impression that the locations are quite distinct villages. Once again careful drawing will help in the preparation of the locations which will have to be made to *seem* separate in some way.

Re-Modelling

Location interiors often have to be re-modelled or decorated to make them suitable for shooting. One should first seek the permission of the owners to carry out the intended alterations and one will almost certainly have to return the interior to its original state. Jonathan Barry used a location interior for Alex's parents' apartment in *A Clockwork Orange.*

"We eventually selected a fairly suitable flat that was close to the production base and set about re-decorating it to our taste. We had, of course, to pay the owners to go and live somewhere else for a few weeks, and after completing the film we restored the flat to its original state." (*Barry.*)

After finding the location for Blofeld's headquarters in *O.H.M.S.S.* the production company were given permission to use the restaurant on condition that it was *left* exactly as it appeared in the Bond film. The interior was completely re-modelled.

"Inside we found a lot of pillars which, of course, made it impossible to shoot as it was. We devised a cantilevered roof, therefore, to give us greater freedom of movement—it was a marvellous engineering job. We left a few pillars at the owners' request." (*Cain.*)

When preparing the Bamburgh Castle location for *Macbeth,* Wilfrid Shingleton had to create a complete external wall for the castle that matched the stonework of the actual castle.

"Bamburgh was a good location because of its proximity to the sea but it hadn't an imposing gateway and the whole point of the final sequence is the attack and siege of a castle. The castle had, therefore, to be attacked with fireballs etc, and we had to build an outer fortification with a main gate and outer wall using the existing castle as a background. The technical problems involved in reconstructing a castle lie in re-creating convincing stonework. We did this by taking casts of existing stonework and matching colour."

When considering the exterior of Lindisfarne Castle in the same film (Macbeth's castle), Wilfrid Shingleton had the problem of making a rather dull exterior appear more interesting against the skyline.

"We didn't have to do much actual building at Lindisfarne. We decided to build a tower that would break the skyline and use a forced perspective painted section to give some depth. It wasn't a big job but it made all the difference visually." (*Shingleton.*)

Improvised Stages

Improvised stages using locally found materials or buildings can be invaluable on location. Perhaps the most flexible improvisation is the Blow-up Dome Stage.

"We used a blow-up dome stage in Yugoslavia when shooting *Fiddler on the Roof* for the interior of Tevye's house and also Lazar Wolf's house. It was very big—150 feet long by 90 feet wide by 40 feet high—kept up by air pressure. It makes a reasonable shooting stage. When we built Tevye's house interior we built two identical interiors side by side and shipped one back to Pinewood so that the two would match exactly.

"In other films, *Alfred the Great,* for example, we built our own stage and workshops in Ireland. A similar stage was made by Dick Frith on *The Lion,* shot in Kenya. On *Swiss Family Robinson* a stage was built in Tobago out of corrugated iron. I have also built sets in small improvised stages in a school hall in Dublin. Certain interiors can be better shot in this way if one needs to float walls on a location interior set. Much depends on the available money." (*Stringer.*)

Location Props

When props are specially made for location interiors one should ensure that their dimensions will allow them access to the room or building. In *A Clockwork Orange* the props in the opening scene had to be designed for narrow access conditions.

"Some of the more special sets such as, for example, the milk bar, we designed to be built in a location interior. Each of the pieces had to be carried up a staircase and therefore had to be thin and not too long." (*Barry.*)

Using authentic local furniture and smaller props is preferable to using imitation—it is certainly cheaper and often the design quality of the local products will be superior to the imitation.

Charge of the Light Brigade. *Designer Ted Marshall. Carefully chosen props add authenticity to historical reconstructions and are often worth the expense and labour of acquiring them.*

Location Colour

One's approach to the use of colour on location depends very much on the attitude of the Director and the kind of script from which one is working and, of course, personal taste. At a time when *naturalism* is emphasised in the cinema it is uncommon to find anything but natural colours used in a location.

"I certainly do not like the extremes of Antonioni in painting streets red or black. That is falsifying colour, and in these circumstances one has to build up a whole film around particular colours. Basically, therefore, I leave locations very much as I find them and only change things if demanded by the character or portrayed by the action." (*Marshall.*)

Kelly's Heroes. *A good example of how a location can be transformed by good design. Note the transformation of the village square, especially the convincing "new" houses. Designed by Jonathan Barry.*

Reverse Angles

One other important aspect of studio design is the planning of reverse angles.

Reverse angle shots are always useful in giving more visual variety to a sequence, and when planned well they can also have other advantages. Perhaps their chief virtue is in giving space to an essentially tight set. (See also Chapter Seven, "Manipulating Space.") If, for example, one is filming a couple talking in the corner of a room one need only build the corner. However, if one wishes to give the impression that the couple are talking in the corner of a *large* room then the reverse angle shot from the corner shooting back into the other two walls of the room would give the maximum value to the background without its being overpowering. Working carefully from a camera angle one can calculate precisely how much of the background set will be revealed and of course one shouldn't build more than will be seen in the shot.

The dressing of the background should not distract the eye of the audience from the foreground action to the background (unless required by the script).

Although it is often necessary to design for depth in a set, necessitating carefully worked out angles, one can shoot quite deliberately on to a flat wall.

"I can remember one scene in *The Best Years of Our Lives*. Two men were sitting at a table opposite to each other questioning each other's motives. Wyler set the scene up to put the men in profile sitting at the table with a blank wall behind them. Other scenes in the café had been long in depth and the drama in the set-up was its simplicity in contrast to the preceding shots." (*Stringer.*)

Chapter 6
Manipulating Space

Because of the current vogue for location shooting, fewer films are being made in the studios, and greater attention is being given to the design of locations rather than design of studio sets. If film-making is concerned with the art of creating illusions, then the studio based film exploits the full potential of cinema for when one is shooting within the studio everything is illusion, however realistic the set. And yet few Designers are able at present to exploit the full potential of the studio world and they are having to build magnificent sets in actuality as in the Bond films, or make a location set look more untouched than it actually is.

Consequently, less gets built and more of the real world is used. The Designer is not asked to compress actual space into something smaller. The neglect of these traditional techniques of creating illusions of space is in some respects surprising since one always has to work as economically as possible and perspective always gives more to the image because with it one can create so many illusions.

Camera Angles
At the very beginning of the process of planning a studio set, the Designer will supply the Director with a number of camera angles. This will help the Director at an early stage to estimate what he will get from the various

sketches that he will have been given. One can work backwards from the plan and elevation of a sketch using a particular lens and one can work out very precisely what will appear on screen after shooting with that particular lens. This process of layout of angles is done in co-operation with the Director and the Cameraman.

The Lens Angle and Perspective

The lens angle is the factor determining what will be recorded in the camera. If one is using a 25mm lens one will have a wide field of view; if one uses a 50mm lens, in plan one will get a narrow field of view, making any room in which one is shooting appear very flat on the screen. This flatness can be counteracted by careful set design. For example, the cameraman may be shooting a close-up with a 50mm lens and by bringing the top of the set down he will achieve a more dramatic composition. Naturally one has to bear in mind that one cannot perspectivise the furniture, nor can one do too much about the floor—it cannot be cheated "up" because the actors have to use it. When sketching one tends to sketch the angle that one can really see— the cone of vision that is about sixty degrees.

If one wishes to use a 35mm lens having an angle of view of, say, ninety degrees, then lines are going to enter the picture area at a sharper angle and the set automatically assumes a diamond shape in plan. One may not want this to happen and therefore by dropping the ceiling lines one can counter the distorting effect of the lens.

Alan Withy comments on practical problems faced when he designed the fire engine showroom set in the film *Go to Blazes:*

"I once designed a set to have the feeling of being large—far larger than I could afford to build—and I wanted the actors to use it in depth. I first made a perfectly consistent initial sketch of what I wanted on the set, taking everything down to the proper eye-level. I then decided to perspectivise the set but on an artificial basis whereby everything would converge to a point on the studio floor. In this case, everything—the office on the left, the lettering on the windows, the rubber plants—was taken down in perspective until the back wall in fact came to only one foot six inches in height. The spiral staircase which nobody was required to use is a scenic painted cut-out so arranged that it touches only a small area of floor. It is a perfectly straightforward scene-painting, worked out inch to the foot on the drawing board and then enlarged. The fire engines were made as a series of cut-outs. The ceiling is made as a single piece—painted as wood strip planks in perspective. The fire engines in the foreground were in fact genuine with painted cut-outs simulating other engines in the background. Everything except these real fire engines was perspectivised consistently. This meant that when we photographed the set it appeared that the eyeline was near the bottom of the picture giving the effect of a low-angle shot. The actual camera level was the normal eyelevel of roughly four feet six inches." (*Withy.*)

Shooting against Perspective

Since a perspectivised set has been built from the viewpoint of one camera position, one might imagine that shooting within that set would be restricted to that single camera position. In fact one has a great deal of freedom in the

FACIA IN FOREGROUND "FIRE APPLIANCE MANUFACTURERS"

FIRE EXTINGUISH

INTERIOR FIRE ENGINE SHOWROOMS

Set sketch for the fire engine showroom in Go to Blazes *designed by Alan Withy.*

choice of set-ups so long as one is always taking the perspective into account. Again using the fire engine showroom as an example, Alan Withy comments on the problems of shooting against the perspective in the set.

"There was no restriction on the Director as long as he kept within the area of the real objects. Wherever the camera pointed it saw convincing shapes. The disadvantage of shooting reverse shots was not very apparent. One could, in fact, photograph any part of these offices from any angle, but one had to accept that if one shot it straight on it looked as if one were still seeing it obliquely. When shot completely the wrong way round things did not distort too badly to be unacceptable. The lines would part a little of course and I could see it because I knew what was happening; but in principle one can get away with shooting against perspective as long as the convergence point of the perspective is well behind the camera. If one placed the camera at the point of convergence then it would look very odd but it is most unlikely that one would need to put the camera in that position. There is also a tendency when shooting level to have more ceiling in frame than one would normally expect at that angle but this does not usually restrict the Director." (*Withy.*)

91

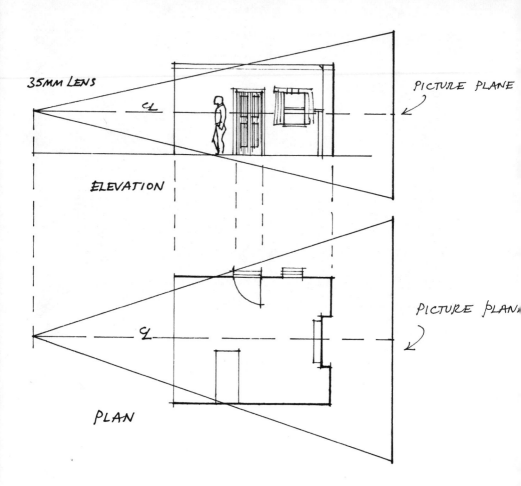

35MM LENS

CL

PICTURE PLANE

ELEVATION

PICTURE PLAN.

CL

PLAN

Projecting a Set Up Sketch from a Plan and Elevation
Having drawn up the Plan and Elevation of the set to scale, place the Elevation of the set above the Plan, and lay the selected lens angle on to the drawing. Sketch in the action figure of one of the characters in the script. At any suitable point draw the Picture Plane line.

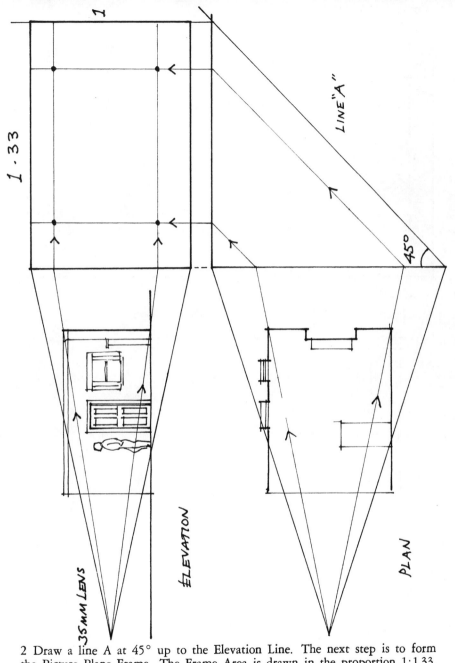

2 Draw a line A at 45° up to the Elevation Line. The next step is to form the Picture Plane Frame. The Frame Area is drawn in the proportion 1:1.33. Draw lines from the centre of the lens through the drawing of the Plan and Elevation and carry them through into the Picture Frame. Where the lines cut across each other is the beginning of the projected picture.

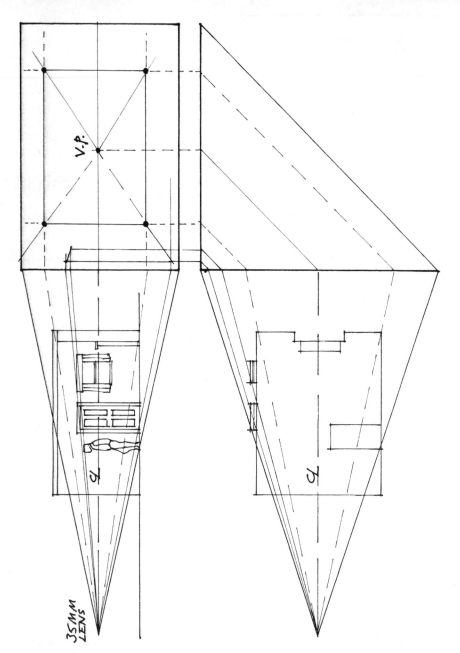

3 Draw the centre line CL through the picture frame and form the Vanishing Point where the lines intersect. Continue to project lines through from the Plan and Elevation and form more projected images on the Picture Frame.

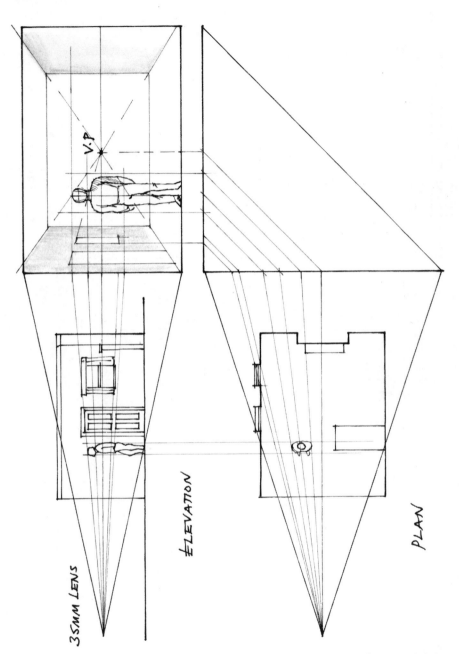

V.P.

35MM LENS

ELEVATION

PLAN

4 Project the figure in the Elevation and Plan (established at six feet in height) —of course if one knows the actual height of the actor it will make the projected sketch more authentic. Begin to add tone to the sketch and fill in more details.

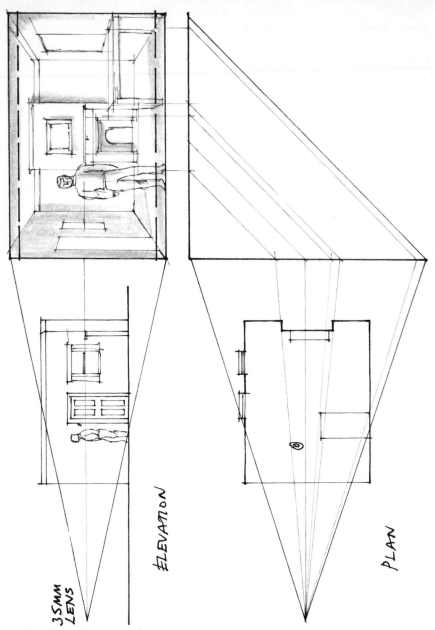

ELEVATION

35MM LENS

PLAN

5 Complete the set-up sketch and fill in details of dressing, colour, tone, as necessary. From this sketch one can get a very clear idea of what the camera will photograph from that angle. It will also show what area the set and camera will need when planning stage or location lay-outs. The broken lines show the 1:1.75 screen ratio and the area of cut-off which will not be seen if the finished film is projected with this screen ratio.

A good example of a furnished colour sketch. The colour values in the set are carefully worked out so as to give as much help as possible to the Set Dresser and Costume Designer. From The Prince and the Pauper. *Designed by Michael Stringer.*

Two quite different approaches to colour. Above: *The* naturatistic *approach is in fact only superficially naturatistic. The colour and the props are very carefully selected and arranged. From* Rally (*Finland*). Below: *Highly subjective emotive use of colour in* Repeat with Us the Following Exercise (*Brazil*).

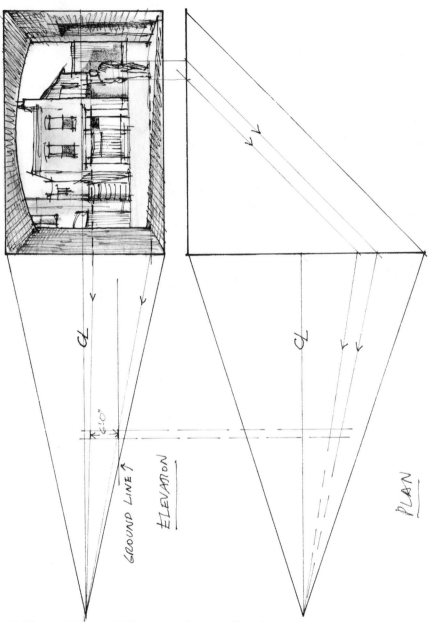

Making a Plan and Elevation from a Sketch

Set up the chosen lens in Plan and Elevation and take any point in the sketch that one knows has a dimension. In this instance one can use the man who is six feet tall and the lines are run back to the Picture Plane until they scale at six feet in the Elevation Plane. Draw the ground line and establish the scale of the man.

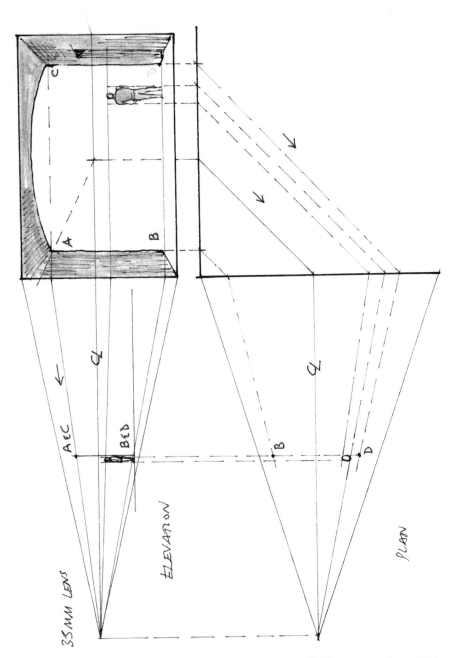

2 Continue to return the lines back to the Plan and Elevation and establish lines AB and CD.

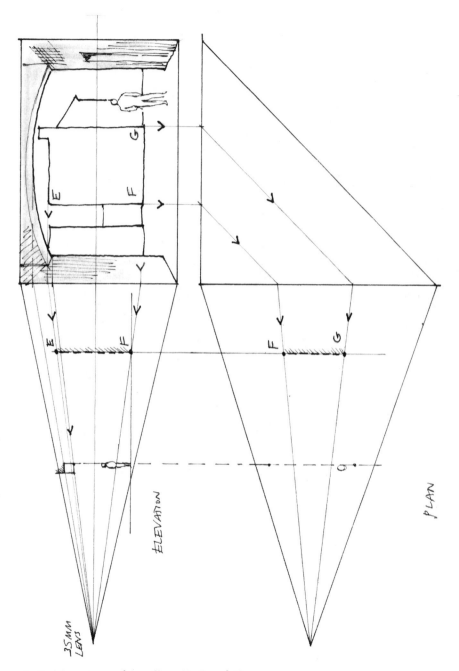

3 Continue to mark up lines E, F and G.

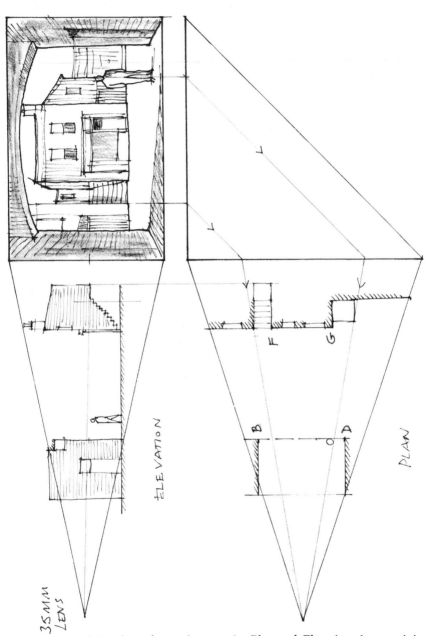

4 Having established the key points on the Plan and Elevation the remaining windows, doors and steps can be quickly sketched in on the drawing. One will now know exactly what sort of set one will build from the sketch as seen from the one camera point.

Two views of the completed fire engine showroom including the painted flat "staircase" and the reduced scale fire engines. The camera can move around quite easily within the perspectivised area.

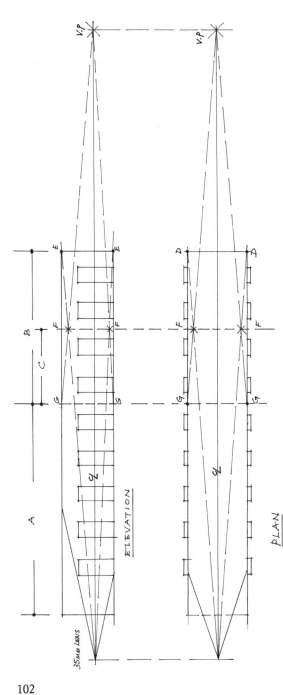

ELEVATION

PLAN

35MM LENS

Forced Perspective

If one wishes to give the impression of a long corridor and one is restricted in stage space it is often necessary to *Force* the *Perspective* of the set by means of building a Forced Perspective section of the set. At the end of this Forced Perspective section one can carry on the illusion of depth by placing a Painted Backing in the correct position.

Method

Having decided on the length of actual corridor to be built, draw an imaginary extension of the corridor at any length necessary (section B). Decide on the section into which one will *Force* the imaginary corridor. Establish the Camera height and then draw the Centre Line (CL).

Draw a line from point E and point D back to the camera lens point and mark its intersection with Plane F.

Draw lines from point G through points F and where each line hits the centre line of the camera one will locate the Vanishing Point (VP).

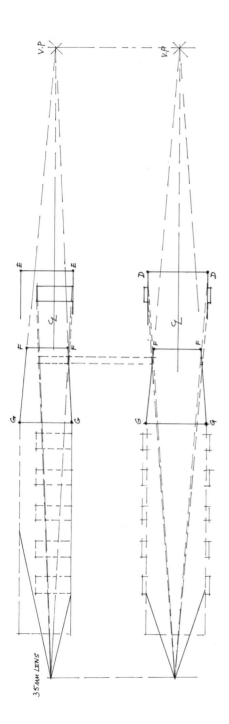

2 The Forced Perspective area and the Vanishing Point of the Perspective have been established. Draw lines back to the camera lens point from the farthest door on the Plan and Elevation of the Imaginary Corridor. Where these lines hit the Forced Perspective section we establish the first "perspectivised" door.

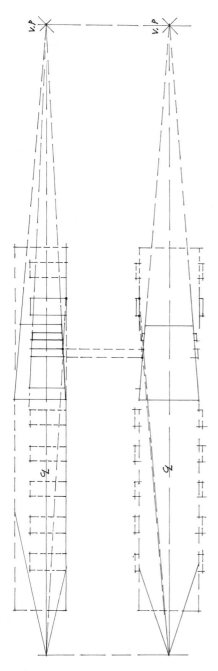

3 Having established the one perspective door on Plan and Elevation continue the process until all the doors are drawn up. One will find that by connecting the tops of the door with the Vanishing Point all lines will automatically follow towards the Vanishing Point, and the completed Forced Perspective will be perfect.

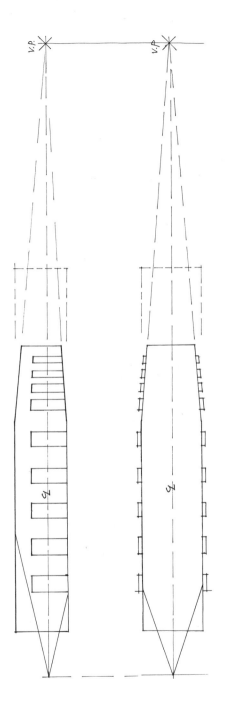

4 It should be noted that the only perfect angle on the set will be from the camera position lined up with the Vanishing Point height and plan position. The camera can track and pan within these limitations. Assuming the Director and the Cameraman understand these calculated positions the result on the screen will be satisfactory and correct.

105

Building Reverse Angle Sets

One way of overcoming the problem of reverse angles is to build reverse angle sets, i.e. that part of the main set that will appear in the reverse angle shot. The set would generally have to be of normal perspective otherwise the shots would not cut with the master take within the perspectivised set, although one could build for the reverse angle in perspective if it were justified.

The Actor in a Perspectivised Set

Putting actors into a perspectivised set will not create problems so long as one avoids obvious mistakes. If one were able to see somebody in one shot walk the full distance from the foreground to background one might detect something wrong. But just as it is difficult to analyse the perspective line of a corner, a dado, and a floor with one's eye then it is just as difficult to analyse perspective in the relationship between the actor and the set. Of course, one could work it out on paper but the audience is dependent on what the effect is *visually*. The Director, therefore, has a large measure of freedom.

There may be occasions when one wishes to put an actor into an obviously distorted set. The reason may be to heighten tension (as in a horror film), or it may be done in a television commercial to attract attention. In the illustration from a commercial set, Alan Withy created deliberate distortion by throwing columns inwards to achieve a rather lyrical feeing in a dancing sequence.

"We were trying to simulate the distortion of an extremely wide-angle lens in the set, enabling us to shoot the action with a standard lens. We had a very restricted space and we had to put across a feeling of depth and space using a normal lens. The vanishing point of the vertical lines is somewhere above. What we were after was a couple of normal looking people dancing in a distorted set. The length of the set was perhaps eighteen or twenty feet. The columns were restrained with piano wire and the rest was drapery on a leaning framework." (*Withy.*)

Although considerable amounts of money are often available for the making of commercials there are many occasions when economics force the Designer to create ingenious solutions to his design problems. Alan Withy describes two occasions on which he had very restricted space in which to develop intriguing "commercial" situations:

"We did the Ronson commercial in Goldhawk studios in a small water tank. The smaller of their stages has a sunken area twenty feet long. We had to have the water rising, which was impractical in the time we had for shooting. After all, one cannot put in a thousand gallons from the local supply and then take it out if the Director wants a re-take. The script required the water to be slowly rising with the men tied to the metal rings.

"We made a forced perspective because of lack of space and lack of money. It was also the only way in which we could control the water. We couldn't in fact raise the water so the obvious solution was to lower the set. The set, therefore, was built quite small and put on tubular runners and it was merely lowered down to the desired water level. It was easily enough adjusted at any time. Everything was built in perspective.

"In another sequence a man leaves a cell; he goes down a corridor and up to a door; he knocks and enters the room. I worked the shot out and decided that I needed a camera height of only two inches over the top of the step.

The illusion of a long hall contained in a set only a few feet deep. The background is miniaturised to scale and the steps to the right of frame are tapered planks. Designed by Alan Withy.

I needed to build a half door (that is all that was seen); and after passing through the door the man walks into the forced perspective of the corridor. He walks down this corridor for only two or three paces and then we cut to a high angle shot of his feet. The door at the end of the corridor, therefore, was built no more than one foot six inches high and the rest of the corridor was forced into that extreme perspective. The wall at left was built solid as was the lamp, while the steps on the right were wooden strips tapering in width from seven inches to three inches. The arches were painted cut-outs, and within three feet the scale is reduced drastically." (*Withy.*)

Models and Perspective

If one has to devise a convincing set in an extremely restricted space one may decide to make use of models in addition to one "normal" set with actors. In the *Turkish Delight* commercials some real space was used but great use was made of models. Beyond the real action Alan Withy designed a number of deep visual recesses using photo cut-outs, in a variety of sizes. An oriental fantasy was required and this enabled the design team to play with perspective.

"We began by shooting up into some domes and arches. The camera moved down from the dome on to the armed guard. The domes were made quite small with the decorative centre-piece a paper doyly. The original design was drawn out in perspective to give a feeling of flowing movements down the

107

Turkish Delight *commercial. A good example of the use of a miniature set using life size people. The door is a foreground miniature placed in front of the camera lens.*

dome then into the room through the gates. The diameter of this dome section was only three feet and the gates were virtually a foreground miniature. They had to be wide enough to let the camera through but no wider. We were merely devising a method whereby we could get to the couple who were disposing of the product and how one did it was mainly a matter of arousing interest by using interesting shapes and obviously finding the right props.

"The fact that the gates are miniatures is not revealed in their relationship to the people, because during the tilt of the camera no people appear on screen. As one approaches the door the people are hidden behind, so one is able to shoot against the perspective quite successfully. The people only appear as the camera gets so close to the door as to make it appear life-size. The pattern of arches again gives a feeling of great depth as we move into the room. Beyond the arches are the cut-out photographs of the guards in varying sizes to give scale to the perspective background." (*Withy.*)

That Kind of Woman *Alan Withy's perspectivised studio reconstruction of a location exterior.*

Studio Reconstruction of Locations

It is of course standard practice to re-create locations in the studio when it is more desirable for one reason or another to shoot in the studio rather than on the actual location. Such studio sets may be built to the natural size but often the limitations of the studio set make it necessary to build the studio reconstruction in a false perspective.

One such studio reconstruction is illustrated above; it is a reconstruction of the "London Apprentice," a public house in the Isleworth district of London.

To the right is a church and a graveyard; to the left a river. The script required a houseboat to be moored with quite a long sequence of night shooting. This created an immediate problem because the water was tidal and of course shooting at night meant extra expense. It was decided, therefore, to shoot on a stage about 118 feet long.

The area of the action is full size. To give the impression of the path running slightly upwards, the set is running very slightly *down*wards. The maximum available area of tank was used and the mooring posts were designed around the tank. The boat was put in full size and level. The near posts are full size but the further ones are much shorter to force the perspective.

The buildings at the rear of the set are painted cut-outs. A police car that drives into the set at the rear in front of the pub was in fact a model car about one foot high. All the painted cut-outs were to a forced perspective running away from the camera.

"The secret with this sort of work is to organise the normal set and the transitions to the perspective so that they merge harmoniously. As long as the set is designed to fit the action with the perspectivised sections put well into the background, then one can shoot the action from virtually any angle that one requires." (*Withy.*)

109

Stages in the construction of perspectivised mountain stronghold for Where Eagles Dare. *Designed by Peter Mullins. The completed castle stood only sixty feet from the set floor.*

Sketch of the Russian Army by Ted Marshall for Charge of the Light Brigade. *In the actual shooting many of the soldiers were in fact cardboard cut-outs.*

Location Communications

The Designer should ensure that communications between himself and the rest of the unit and the unit and the Art Department are always open. On major productions a large Art Department can only work effectively if all members are kept in contact with each other. On smaller productions one can only work economically on location if one has access to an efficient communication system. Michael Stringer outlines his approach to location communications:

"We had a mobile sound van in direct telephone link with the production office in Zagreb. We used a big transport fleet of Volkswagens and Jeeps, which had to be bought, plus the transport of all the equipment-generators, lights, etc.

"On remote locations I would certainly have walkie-talkies or telephone to keep a link with the production office even down to motorola car radios—we used these once on a film shooting in Israel. I would also hope that we were not based more than twenty miles from our base workshop so that once one starts shooting, the timber, rostrum tops, and all construction materials, paint, stirrup pumps, or petrol driven spray equipment are available easily and quickly." (*Stringer.*)

112

Chapter 7
Studio Design

Although many films are being made on location either entirely or in part, films are still being shot in studios and the studio environment offers certain advantages to the Designer. These advantages of equipment and personnel can be a great help to the young Designer, as Peter Mullins explains:

"I prefer to work in a studio. One is surrounded by the expertise of the various departments and it is so easy to communicate with them. On location there is usually only the construction manager at hand to help you out of your difficulties. A good construction manager can be a great help but even so one has to make a lot of compromises because facilities normally available in the studio are lacking." (*Mullins.*)

The Designer in the studio builds his design from the bare walls of the studio; on location the Designer has to start with what the location offers so that by a process of adaptation and selection he can fulfil the requirements of the script and satisfy the Director. It would be a mistake to assume that designing a studio set is very much more difficult than the location set. Because of the factors mentioned above the Designer may feel free to design in a setting that is minimal. In the studio the Designer can have complete control of everything that appears on the set—he rarely has this control on location. This control can be very useful in films having a strong element of fantasy and action:

"On Bond films one has to do an enormous amount of trickwork and one can only do it in the studio. In *Diamonds* the whole elevator sequence was built up in the studio. We took the first shot at the bottom of an elevator in Las Vegas. In the final shot where Bond hangs up at the top of the skyscraper, it was all studio-shot. It looks ten times more effective than reality even if we had risked the artist's life and shot it on location. The fight in the lift is another example. At first one might be tempted to think that one could find an old fashioned lift that would be suitable, but a little thought would bring home to you that it could not possibly be done. A lift is say five feet by three feet— too small for a camera, let alone people and action. We had to build this as a studio set in which the stunt men could fight it out using breakaway glass. Also we could control the up and down movements of the lift to a split second. We rigged a platform on both sides of the lift which could travel up and down with the lift transporting the camera. This amount of control is essential in these situations." (*Adam.*)

Studio Procedure

The procedure followed by the Designer from script to building the set through all the stages of preparation, will depend almost entirely on the type of production and the Director. Thumbnail sketches; continuity sketches; finished set sketches; models etc, may all have to be produced or none may have to be produced. Jonathan Barry, who does very fine continuity drawings, did none on *A Clockwork Orange;* likewise Syd Cain, who is an exceptional draughtsman, had this comment to make on working with Hitchcock:

"When I worked with Hitchcock on *Frenzy* he didn't want any sketches at all since being an ex-Art Director himself he was able to visualize each set-up. I gave him a lay-out of where the main camera angles would be. These he either approved immediately, or suggested minor changes; that is all I had to do. I didn't have to make any cardboard models. One could always depend on him to know exactly what he wanted. If we had a room, for example, with just two walls, that is all I would have to build. There was no need to build the other two walls as one invariably has to do with other directors. Most directors usually say that they do not need extra walls, but then they come on set and decide to shoot a reverse angle. You can then expect a big panic while extra walls are built for one or two shots. With Hitchcock if he asks for two walls you can be sure that is all he needs." (*Cain.*)

Re-Use of Sets (Re-Vamping)

Obvious economies can be made by using sets or parts of sets that have been built for other films. Although some studios are tending to do away with scene docks as an unnecessary expense (on the premise that it is cheaper to build inexpensive sets for low budget productions rather than employ expensive labour to look after scene docks that take up valuable space) companies that usually produce films within one *genre* (for example the British company, Hammer) often keep parts of a set that can be easily adapted for use in another film.

For some years Hammer have specialised in economically produced horror films, many of them designed by Scott MacGregor. One example of the way a basic unit can be adapted to many other films is illustrated opposite and above.

An initial set was built for the film *Taste the Blood of Dracula.* The set was

Taste the Blood of Dracula. *Church interior set designed by Scott MacGregor.*

a huge church and the illustrations are of the east window and the west door. The building of the church took a substantial proportion of the art department budget.

This original set was used in a modified form on a number of subsequent Hammer productions including *Vampire Lovers, Horrors of Frankenstein* and *Scars of Dracula.*

Vampire Lovers *The* Blood of Dracula *set after re-vamping.*

In the film *Vampire Lovers* the church underwent a minor reconstruction. The large Gothic window was eliminated, although the vertical recess was kept. The recess is terminated by a lowered arch which stands above a gallery. Most of the other architectural details are kept virtually intact, except for the addition of the gallery at right. The large column to the right of the photograph, for example, is kept as are the small windows to either side of the recess. In *Vampire Lovers* these small windows become openings on the passageway that leads up to the small gallery, the glass being removed from them.

Changes in the rest of this set are limited to the dressing and the lighting. The dressing in *Vampire Lovers* would indicate that the church is decaying and is now unused, at least for normal purposes. More texture has been added to the walls at right. This effect can be most easily achieved by running rivulets of thin plaster down the wall and then adding liberal quantities of dirt.

For *Horrors of Frankenstein* this corner was cleaned up considerably, as can be seen from the above illustration. A staircase has been placed to the left of the set in lieu of the gallery. The arches have been modified with the doorway moved but essentially this is the same corner in *Taste the Blood of Dracula* and *Vampire Lovers*.

The more significant changes again are in the set dressing. In this latter film the dressing would indicate that the house is in use. The lighting, however, as in the two previous illustrations is still used to emphasise the mood of the story.

116

Horrors of Frankenstein *The same set after further re-vamping.*

Reality and Fantasy

The contribution made by the Designer to a studio set often reflects his own character as a creative artist and quite obviously Designers will differ tremendously in their approach to the script. One Designer may think theatrically when given four walls in a studio, another may do his best to re-create the world outside as realistically as possible.

"My principle in film design is always to go a little bit towards the theatrical. To copy reality is not difficult when one has learned the trade. But I do not think this to be the idea of film design. From the audience's point of view I think a reconstructed reality which is partly an expression of the Designer's imagination is more satisfactory. For example, in *Goldfinger* there was the interior of Fort Knox. Of course we weren't allowed to shoot inside Fort Knox; I am sure from the cinematic point of view the interior is very dull. It is just a series of underground passages and rooms. We wanted to pile the gold thirty feet high and put it behind iron grilles. Now in reality gold is not stored in piles of more than two feet but our version of reality at a glance conveyed gold, Fort Knox, and the essence of the identity of the place. We had a lot of letters from viewers asking us how we got into Fort Knox. The audience completely accepted our studio reconstruction.

"On *Dr. Strangelove* we had no co-operation from the American authorities. But to have shot the film at NORAD wouldn't have given that slight tongue in

Somewhat larger than life gold vault for Goldfinger. *Designed by Ken Adam.*

cheek and claustrophobic feeling that I have tried to achieve in the war room with that big circular table with everybody sitting around it as in a poker game. In this case the screenplay demands a kind of reality that belongs to the studio setting." (*Adam.*)

On the other hand Michael Stringer has often found it necessary to capture the essence of a particular location and after careful observation re-create the total atmosphere of location in the studio.

"We had to go to France and photograph villages and shop fronts and a variety of details. We made a great number of drawings and measurements and collected a certain amount of actual signs and general props bought in France and shipped to England. Of course other props we re-created (and it is cheaper to do this). For the next film we were able to re-vamp the whole set into a Scottish village standing on a hillside. This saved a great deal of expense. This kind of set building depends on the Designer being able to steep himself in the atmosphere of a country and then being able to re-create this atmosphere in the studio. All Designers should be able to do this—it being one of the more routine aspects of film design.

"One may bring back just one French roofing tile that can be copied at the studio workshop. The street can be made up of concrete cobbles again made as replicas of an original cobble. The whole set was built on tubular scaffolding since it had to be built on a slope—the slope being an essential part of the action. We needed a hill; in Hollywood they would build a hill with earth but in England tubular scaffolding is used. We used some real interiors for shooting—a café and one of the houses. We re-created the suburban railway

Michael Stringer's studio reconstruction in England of French exterior captures the full flavour of provincial France. The set includes many items of dressing brought over from France to add atmosphere to the set.

on a build-up bank with a cut-out railway train on a converted pit trolley railway line. It was made full size and from a distance it looked like a real train going across the background. We then cut to an actual train shot in Paris and built extensively at Pinewood for that shot. Even big construction in the studio can be cheaper than travelling with the whole crew to shoot something small on location." (*Stringer.*)

"The original intention in *Diamonds Are Forever* was to shoot the entire film on location. The producer and director wanted to use American location interiors and exteriors. I went along with this, although I didn't think it necessarily the best way of doing a Bond film. At a later stage it was decided for financial reasons to transfer many of the exterior sets into the studio. On a film like a Bond, which is something of a visual extravaganza, unless you are fortunate enough to find the most incredible location interiors I think it better to design the film in the studios. There are no rules about it of course." (*Adam.*)

Designing Fantasy

Another *genre* of fantasy film which normally requires the control obtainable in the studio setting is space fiction. The narrative content of the space film is often minimal and the impact of the film often depends on superbly finished sets which are convincing representations of future design. Materials must be capable of very fine finish unlike, for example, horror films.

"The chief difference between designing for horror films and designing futuristic fantasy is in terms of materials. In horror films one tends to use lots of plaster and masses of dirt and you can give lots of atmosphere and character to the set. In the futuristic type of production you have to produce a very polished job. It is no good, for example, trying to imitate steel by using painted plywood. It will look awful. One can use wood but it has to be rubbed down and filled with alabastine before spraying with silver nitrate, or finished in graphite. It is possible to get away with a certain amount of bad workmanship in horror films but never on a modern set." (*MacGregor.*)

Scott MacGregor explains some other aspects of his design for *Moon Zero Two*:

"The exterior of the space reception area was based on the work of the architect Candela. We started with the exterior and the space ship arrival location. We then had to build the connecting tunnel to this underground reception area. From here the mono-rail would take passengers to the moon Hilton.

"The interior of the reception area would on earth be made of concrete but I wanted to give a much lighter effect and used some translucent fabric stretched over the strengthening struts, made of tubular aluminium. We selected Swedish furniture but one is really taking a risk putting *any* furniture on to the moon. The floor was paper on stretched burlap hessian. We then stuck two layers of craft paper over the hessian. It was painted white and then varnished. It was perfectly good for ten days' wear. The costumes were mainly silvery grey. In space we used a variety of colours so that the audience could identify the characters. For some reason we felt that without giving specific characters distinctive coloured costumes the audience would have difficulty identifying with them in space.

"We conceived the Hilton Hotel as being cut out of rock—it was in effect an enormous cavern. The impression we wanted to give was that the hotel should be cut out of a mountain. The floor, for example, was given a polished stone finish which I based on agate crystal. The horizontal surfaces were meant to be highly polished agate and the rough sections on the vertical surfaces carried the colour and texture of agate crystal. All the surfaces were built up on wood covered with plaster. We had to make a clay model of this enormous shape on the studio floor. Some of the technicians wanted to make the cast in two halves but I didn't really think that would work. So we made the cast from a one-piece mould. The cast was then shellacked and sprayed with gold paint to give a high polish. The windows had to tilt so as to give no reflection. Outside views were simply painted backing. The moon shape was fibreglass with an internal light source. There had to be something of a vulgar feeling about the whole place since the Hotel was frequented by vulgar people most of the time.

"There was a dancing area in the middle where there were floor shows. Sometimes there was a 'Wild-West Night,' sometimes a 'Mexican Night,'

Moon Zero Two. *Designed by Scott MacGregor. Reception area (see text opposite)*.

so we had phony cactus plants standing around—and it had to *look* phony too. The screens in the wall had kinetic light displays on them. The screen was made of varnished cartridge paper. Behind, two *brutes* illuminated revolving discs of perspex with paint splashed on them giving continually changing colours.

"The walls were made of plaster with a roof in fibreglass. The dome had to be suspended on a chain since it would not rest safely on the supporting walls.

"The upper floor was reached by way of a lift. The bedrooms were also designed as if cut out of rock. The windows faced the moon's surface. The rooms were made very simply with chicken wire and wood support with plaster just trowelled on very roughly to give a pleasant texture.

"The basic idea came from the film *Action of the Tiger* in which I designed some caves based on real caves in southern Spain near Gaudix. In that district we found peasants actually living in caves which had been electrified and

121

Moorish room from Taste the Blood of Dracula *(see below). Designed by Scott MacGregor.*

made as comfortable as possible. The action in our film took place in Albania but I liked the basic idea of using the Spanish caves as a model for them. And eventually the same caves in Spain became a model for the moon Hilton.

"The moon repair shop was meant to be out on the desert of the moon's surface. Entry was through the airlock. Originally I intended to make one of Buckminster Fuller's domes with translucent walls. But this would have cost too much. In the end I used two inch by one inch wood strip for support and it looked very good. The cameraman didn't put any light through it. He simply lit the white backing behind and the reflected light filtered through into the dome itself. The panels were made from extruded plastic—a very inexpensive and rapid process." (*MacGregor.*)

Sets Based on Drapes and Dressing
Effective studio sets can be devised without necessarily having to build. One can achieve convincing effects with the help of drapes and dressing. In *Taste the Blood of Dracula* Scott MacGregor had to create a set depicting the east end of London in Victorian times. Part of the action took place in a soup kitchen run by a philanthropist who, by some quirk of nature, had an interest in more exotic amusements. Behind the soup kitchen he kept a brothel, having a number of rooms of varying *décor.*

"There was a Moorish room with snake dances. This set was very simple indeed and nothing was actually built. All I did was to put up some flats,

122

Mirrors can be used effectively to create space on a small set. Taste the Blood of Dracula. *Designed by Scott MacGregor.*

cover them with drapes and then dress the set with Moorish furniture behind which I put Moorish screens. The screens were made of a lattice that builds up in sections—it is in common use in Cairo and other middle eastern cities as window shutters." (*MacGregor.*)

Lit well, this kind of set is totally convincing because it has a rich visual texture that conveys the desired atmosphere to the audience. This type of set is also very economical to erect as the only costs involved are the props. There is no labour to hire and no construction materials to purchase.

Creating Space with Mirrors

The Designer is always encountering the problem of having to make a small space appear much bigger than in fact it is. This can occur on a location in which case the Designer may be limited in what he can do beyond advise a wide-angle lens and compose his set dressing to give the illusion of depth.

In the studio other devices can be used and Scott MacGregor describes how on one occasion he was legitimately able to use mirrors to good effect:

"The Oscar Wilde set was very small but we were able to give an enhanced feeling of space by using mirrors. We were trying to re-create the effect of the grill room at the Café Royal. In reality the columns are much higher but for the film, we cheated. If we had shot them life-size we would have to have shot from so far away as to have ruined the visual effect we wished to achieve. Luckily I knew the Café very well—I had been so often since coming to London as a child. During the research for the scene I examined paintings of the Café that had been done during the period in which the film was set. Orpen's painting of the Café is probably the best known but there are others.

"The columns and caryatids were already built in the studio and we easily made the seats and made a beautiful replica of the original menu card." (*MacGregor.*)

123

The gauze shot 1. An inexpensive way of effecting a transition from one set to another. The technique is derived from the theatre and is used above and opposite by Scott MacGregor in Vampire Lovers.

Theatrical Techniques

Sometimes techniques used commonly in the theatre can be employed in the cinema and are especially useful if economies have to be made. One such technique is the gauze shot—the means whereby one can zoom through a wall from one set into another.

To prepare for a shot in *Taste the Blood of Dracula,* two sets were built side by side on the studio floor. The technique described by Scott MacGregor enabled the director to effect an interesting transition from one set to another without using opticals.

"In the story it was necessary for one girl to look through the wall to another girl lying in bed. (She was able to do this because she was a vampire and evidently vampires can do this sort of thing.) We could have done the transition in the lab, but the laboratory dissolves take time and are an expense, so we decided on a gauze shot.

"For this we needed a painting over the bed and the Scene Painter, Bob White, did a beautiful "Boucher" in three days. He also did one on the other side of the same piece of gauze.

"We set up the camera on one side of the gauze with the lights on in the first set and off in the other. As we zoomed in on the Boucher painting we lowered the lights on the first set and raised them on the other set. The painting gradually disappeared and we were able to move in to a big close-up of the girl in the other set. Technically, it was similar to a transformation scene in the theatre." (*MacGregor.*)

The gauze shot 2 (above) and 3 (below).

Working from Photographs

Locations that are to be reconstructed in the studio require a great deal of careful research to ensure accuracy in the reconstruction and if the draughtsmen in the Art Department are to reproduce accurately several photographs of the location will be taken. Often the draughtsman will be given a photograph, and he may have to re-build what is in the photograph without there being any indication of measurements and no indication of the camera angle or indeed the camera height. It may be architecture with a figure standing somewhere and one will hazard a guess at the height of that figure; or there may be some brickwork and one will know that as a rule there are four bricks to the foot.

"From this flimsy information, and the fact that as an architectural subject it is bound to have some perspective lines, one can then locate the vanishing points because one is finding the directions; one is finding a point on the photograph and finding where in plan and elevation that point exists. This is the beginning. Once one has located this point one can build up a reconstruction from that point. One can build every detail that is visible to the camera." (*Withy.*)

Perspective and Architectural Detail

Modern sets with their clean simple lines may not present too much of a problem to construct in perspective if one projects the camera angles correctly. However, period sets can present problems because the lines are not usually so clean—a Baroque banqueting hall may have much embellishment built on to the basic structure. Unless one is careful one may find that one is having to create perspective running in more than one direction.

"The secret is in finding a design in which those things that have to taper do not taper in too many directions at once. In other words one can shape a piece of timber to take it down from four inches to three inches but one does not really want to have a complex section of it which has to be diminished in more than one direction.

"Once I had to build a prison set at M-G-M. I designed a complex cornice and I had to diminish it. It was not too difficult but it was laborious. One has to start by making a section at each end correctly and then making lines connect up. That particular cornice was then only useful in that one place at that one time. This is true of any architectural features that one makes. They apply only to the set for which they were designed and one cannot really put them into the scene dock (of course it often happens that they *are*). One would come with great joy to a lovely window only to discover that, when measured, it would drop a few inches at the top. This would have been fine for the purpose for which it was made, but quite useless for any other set." (*Withy.*)

Chapter 8
Dressing the Set

Dressing should be understood as being part of the process of telling the screen story. It should not be used simply to fill up screen space in a more or less decorative way. Dressing, therefore, has its origins in the characters and in the action. It is related to the characters in that it can tell the audience a great deal about their circumstances—is a man wealthy or poor?—is he a family man?—what is the period of the action, and so on. Dressing is related to the action in that on the set it is integrated into the action. A chair is for sitting on, a table has to be walked around, etc. The dressing has to be appropriate to the action and to the characterisation.

It is imperative that at an early stage the Designer and the Director confer about the characterisation and the action. Both may change or develop as the film proceeds but it is better to be continually adjusting one's ideas about points of dressing than to present the Director with something at rehearsals that has little to do with the characters or the action. Sometimes the situation and characters are fairly clearly defined at the outset and after examining the initial sketches or models the Director may leave the Designer to get on with the set, working with his Dresser and Buyer. Other Directors may, however, be less clear in their mind about how certain characters will develop and it is important to be in constant communication to ensure that one's design is as relevant as possible at any particular stage.

Jonathan Barry describes some of his problems with regards to the action and characters in *A Clockwork Orange.*

"The importance of the set to the dramatic structure of the film is that whatever the Director wishes to say in the scene will be said in the set before it is said in the action. The author's set is very bizarrely dressed and as soon as the audience sees the setting they make up their minds about the kind of people who live in that kind of setting. (In this particular film the audience will quickly decide that nobody they know would live in that setting and come to the speedy conclusion that they are going to have to deal with a couple of original people.)

"This is both the danger and the strength of design in a film. This is the reason why Directors like Kubrick are very concerned to know exactly what is happening. Kubrick makes tremendous efforts to control the design of his films because if he didn't he could easily find himself making a film that he did not fully intend to. Particularly in a subject like *A Clockwork Orange,* in which there are so many variables that demand very many creative decisions. In a film like *Spartacus,* however, there is a limit to how far one can stray from one standard rendering of the subject, at least in visual terms." (*Barry.*)

One difficult design problem in *A Clockwork Orange* lay in the characterisation of Alex and his relationship with his parents.

"There was a variety of design elements used and in a way they might not have seemed compatible; for example, the opening café scene which was very futuristic compared with the interior of Alex's parents' flat. But there was little in the film that does not already exist somewhere in London at the present time. The design impact stemmed from a careful selection of ready-made units, taken from the normal setting in which we see and understand them, put together in a completely new setting.

"With the parents' apartment we tried to project the degeneration of modern design to a further degeneracy in the near future. I was also trying to hide the fact that the architecture of the flat that we used was extremely conventional and dull. Not only was it not in the future but it was at least fifteen years in the past!

"I tried to make the colour as strident as possible in an attempt to render the flat ugly. I don't think I succeeded, indeed, I think I made it look too interesting. It was an effort to design the ill-informed taste of intellectually deprived people who rely on commercial interest to form their tastes." (*Barry.*)

Having given some definition to the parents Barry then had to define Alex who, although the product of his parents and having many similar values, was at the same time possessed of several unique features. The design of his bedroom had to reflect this separation. There was another difficulty in that the Alex of the book lacked a clearly defined personality. One of the most impressive aspects of Malcolm McDowell's performance was that he took an essentially two-dimensional character and gave it believable depth.

"If we had given him a misguided interior similar to that given to his parents he wouldn't have been Alex as we know him. He would not succumb to corporate pressures. Also it was necessary to separate him *visually* from his parents. His activities were not those of his parents and we wanted to reflect this in his room.

"This separation we did quite graphically, by giving him a combination lock on his door. It was seen in close-up at the beginning of the film. It was

Above: *Muted colour for the* Zee & Co *set, designed by Peter Mullins, serves as an effective foil to the colourful characterisation of Elizabeth Taylor.* Below: *The mood of a scene can be quickly established by the selection of an overall colour value. In the sketch a sombre scene in* Macbeth *is sensitively portrayed by Wilfrid Shingleton.*

Highly stylised use of colour in John Bodimeade's sketch for a set-up in Casino
Royale. *Designed by Michael Stringer.*

Zee & Co. Dressing extending from character. Note how cleverly each item of décor and dressing has its starting point in Miss Taylor's hairstyle which in turn is an expression of her turbulent character. Designed by Peter Mullins.

assumed that he was a thief so we could explain many of the contents of the room as the spoils of his shop-lifting; his Hi-Fi, his records, and of course the case underneath the bed into which he dropped a thick roll of banknotes and a drawer in which he keeps a number of watches." (*Barry.*)

Changes in the accent given to certain scenes may lead to drastic changes in the dressing of a set and this can cause practical problems.

"The author's house had been dressed, and during rehearsals Kubrick decided that the house had to be completely re-dressed. Kubrick changed the accent of the scene and we had to re-furnish over a weekend to meet the new requirements. I showed Kubrick the catalogue of a modern furniture exhibition which by this time had been dismantled and was scattered in various stores throughout England. We had to send numerous vans to collect the several individual pieces. In the end we shot in a simply furnished room." (*Barry.*)

Because Kubrick likes to be presented with as many compositional options as possible the interior milk bar set at the beginning of the film was designed to be assembled in a variety of ways.

"Kubrick likes to explore every compositional possibility so interiors were built to give countless different possible arrangements in colour and dressing. The set was rather like a big Meccano set with elements of figures; of lettering; of wigs; and of pedestals for the figures. The bases were built to a hexagonal plan to enable us to group them in a multiplicity of ways." (*Barry.*)

Kubrick also wanted as many options as possible in the dressing of the author's house in preparation for the meal scene.

"We had six tables of differing styles at which Malcolm McDowell could have his meal; there were six sets of chairs and dressing that ranged from very ornate black plates and gold knives and forks, to very simple glass plates or white plates. The whole range of possibilities was there from which Kubrick could choose." (*Barry.*)

In contrast to the problems of *A Clockwork Orange* arising out of its unique characterisation and near future period the characters in *Sitting Target* are more orthodox in style and the design problems a little more straightforward.

Jonathan Barry had to design an apartment that would convey the feeling of having been lived in by two quite different people in succession.

"We wanted to give the apartment the feeling that it had been for an older woman and that the man had tired of the original occupant and replaced her by a younger and more trendy occupant. Under the swinging dressing there had to be the remains of a conventional kept woman's apartment.

"The apartment also had to look erotic and be on two levels so that the man and women could hide upstairs when another character came into the house. They had to see him without they themselves being observed. I put mirrors everywhere; ceilings; bedroom; bathroom; using little mosaic mirrors. We also put mirrors down the staircase so that we could see the man's fall reflected in lots of small mirrors. When using mirrors on the set one has always to hinge them so that one can get the camera out of shot if it appears in one of the mirrors." (*Barry.*)

If one has to project the idea of great age in one's dressing it is often useful to use objects that are authentically old. During the early period of planning when one is doing one's research it is useful to keep a note of any old buildings that are to be demolished or other props of suitable age that can be used effectively. *Fiddler on the Roof* presented many examples of genuine old articles used on the set along with studio imitations.

"I had to keep a good eye for old timbers. We built on to the village of Mala Gorica. The synagogue, the shops and the blacksmith's shop were all built with materials retrieved from old buildings that had been pulled down. We made sure that the roofs and the buildings sagged to make them look as if they had been standing there for years. We also took a great deal of care to get the painting and texturing right. Dressing the set was very important and Peter Lamont, our Set Dresser, spent a great deal of time acquiring horses and carts and going into houses asking the tenants if they were willing to exchange their old tables and chairs for new plastic ones.

"It had originally been our intention to get an Ark from a synagogue in Romania and use that. This proved too expensive, so we built our own Ark and aged it carefully to give it the look of a village craftsman's work.

"As a general rule it is much cheaper to use the real thing if possible than making an imitation. But we did make Tevye's pony trap at Pinewood and managed to weather it down beautifully." (*Stringer.*)

Ken Adam has come to a similar conclusion:

"In *Diamonds Are Forever* I designed much of the penthouse furniture myself and it was eventually sold. Some props are much cheaper bought from a shop. We had to buy some metal-framed windows for one scene and we obtained them for a price much lower than anything we could have produced in the studio using any of the available methods. One tends to do this more and more.

"Today it is terribly important to know what goes on in industry. One must know what is available as ready-mades. And believe me, there is still enough work left for the film craftsman." (*Adam.*)

Dressing to evoke period. Jonathan Barry's design for Decline and Fall.

Dressing Procedure

The set will be dressed after the Designer has conferred with the Director and after he has thoroughly acquainted himself with the action. This means that the Designer will be present at rehearsals so that he can make up a ground plan from which to design his dressing.

"In dressing the set I do not look through the lens until a late stage. The script gives me an idea of the action and of course I am around to see where the action takes place during the rehearsal. After this one dresses by instinct. The questions of height of furniture and the relationship of pictures to wall space one feels intuitively. One roughs things out first but one should be prepared to change things about if the overall effect doesn't quite work during the shooting." (*Marshall.*)

The Set and Lighting

For practical design purposes the set is a collection of shapes, colours, and textures. The way in which they are revealed on screen is of vital importance. The method used to reveal them is by lighting the set. Therefore, at a very early stage in set planning the type of lighting will have to be decided upon.

"Kubrick lights a set with the real lights as far as possible and keeps the lights in frame. One doesn't normally have this problem with other Directors. If one is going to dress ordinary lamps into a set one has to be very careful.

Where Eagles Dare *Salt making an effective substitute for snow.*

One should find out what lighting value they have, or whether they can be used with photoflood etc." (*Barry.*)

"We have to decide at the beginning of the set building process where the light source is going to be. We need to know the character of the lighting— is it to be a night shot or a day shot?—and the type of lighting—electricity or oil etc? If shooting on location, one has to know the direction of the sunlight (if there is to be any), and if there will be any bounce light or reflected light." (*Stringer.*)

In *2001: A Space Odyssey* the overall lighting giving no shadow was meant to convey a feeling of indeterminate future. By way of contrast, in lighting Dickens one would use strong shadows with gloss painted walls to impart a shine and glint. Dramatic lighting used with emphatic textures can portray the mood of sombreness or sadness and fear.

Materials

It was during the Sixties that there was more experiment with some of the newer materials.

"By using actual materials you will find that you save a lot on labour costs—an important factor these days. For example, in the old days if you wanted an oak panelled room you would select the wood paper at little cost. You had to prepare your flats very carefully and the paper had to be hung by professional painters. The paper then had to be re-grained since wood grain wall paper always repeated its grain. Nowadays one simply has the wood veneer stuck on to plywood which doesn't cost very much. All that remains

Plaster "cobbles" and "stonework" Greyfriars Bobby. *Designed by Michael Stringer.*

Plaster simulating volcanic lava in The Castaways. *Designed by Michael Stringer.*

Malayan scene on the Pinewood lot in England. Fibreglass palm trees with real palm leaves imported from Malaya for The Castaways. *Designed by Michael Stringer.*

"In the illustration the palm trees were modelled in clay and cast in fibreglass. The fibreglass was wadded to lightweight aluminium tubes on the top of which we had a number of cages into which were slotted real palm fronds specially shipped from Malaya.

"I visited Malaya on a research recce and sent back 500 eighteen foot long palm leaves in crates. We had tried various ways of making eighteen foot palm leaves and considered making vacuum formed leaves but it worked out to be far too expensive. It was much cheaper to import them and in addition we sent back vast quantities of atap, dried palm leaves, knitted together to make the roofs. John Bryan the Producer, and Ronald Neame the Director, both thought it better to shoot the film on the lot at Pinewood in the open air in June rather than to build in the studio." (Stringer.)

134

is the aging. In this way one can save a great deal in labour costs. I felt it important [on the Bond films] to use contemporary material and processes as far as possible. Similar savings can be made on a great number of materials. For example, we have certain processes which allow us to achieve metallic finishes—effect processing—based on silver nitrate, the mirror system—plus very often aluminium or metals with the right finish. Not too long ago we had to use silver paper. As we went along we found that we had fewer and fewer ready made screenplays and more was being left to the creative energies of those in charge of the film to come up with ideas which were then incorporated." (*Adam.*)

The kind of materials used on the set will give the set its predominant character. Plastics and aluminium in a Bond film puts across the hard colourful character of Bond himself and the world in which he moves; natural wood and earth colours used in *Fiddler on the Roof* give a softness to the settings which reflect the warmth of the characters portrayed.

"For the inn interior we used fresh timber and stripped the bark off in the carpenters' shop. We burnt the wood and brushed it before giving it a final waxing. In this way we were able to build a very good Russian style log cabin without having to use plaster. Beams are better done in this way using real timber since one can carve into the wood and get a more effective finish than using plaster for the same job. Plaster casts can become repetitive and too 'oldy worldy' lacking a certain crispness." (*Stringer.*)

In designing *Macbeth* Wilfrid Shingleton also had to strive for a certain kind of realism. Polanski was very anxious to give the set a feeling of "construction," as if the castles were still being built or added to:

"Polanski was very anxious to get a feeling of construction in the images— to make it look as if the castles were in a constant state of being built. So I used quite a lot of timber that seemed newly worked and I had a carpenter with a plane working on many of the surfaces at Dunsinane. Polanski wanted to emphasise reality by portraying the simplicity of life at that time." (*Shingleton.*)

Plaster, being both economical and flexible in its use, is still an extremely popular set building material. Directors tend to prefer to use more modern materials but probably this is mere prejudice, for they may not be so practical for some jobs. Wilfrid Shingleton had the problems of building an exterior wall around Bamburgh Castle and therefore needed a substantial number of building stones which had to be made from casts.

"The casts were made from plaster although originally Polanski had requested fibreglass. Of course for this job fibreglass was out of the question for financial reasons and indeed from the point of view of time. While one is making a single fibreglass cast from a mould one can make ten plaster ones. I assured Polanski that this cheaper method would work so long as we used casts from an actual castle. So we went to Harlech Castle in North Wales and took casts of differing sizes of stone. We found that castles were built with the heavier stones at the base of the walls. As one gets higher smaller stones were used. We got casts of the heavy base stones that were perhaps half the size of a man as well as the different grades of stone from the various levels of Harlech Castle. In this way I was able to reconstruct the visual appearance of a castle quite convincingly." (*Shingleton.*)

Sand casts are very useful in the production of stonework and brickwork.

Effective use of wood and realistic ageing. Oliver! *Designed by John Box.*

"One lays the actual stones in sand and then one uses Vinamould, a rubber compound, to get a good crisp mould for reproduction in plaster mixed with vermiculite." (*Stringer.*)

Plaster was used extensively on *Fiddler on the Roof.* Michael Stringer describes the setting up of the graveyard set.

"The set was highly stylised with twisted trees which were modelled. In fact we made a half inch scale model of the set and employed two Modellers to make scale models of the trees which were then built by the plasterers and metal workers. We had to make several gravestones, with the correct Hebrew lettering. We also had to ensure that the entire set was ready a month before shooting to enable the cast to have the necessary intensive musical rehearsals with the choreographer. All the sets for the film had been built in mock-up form months before shooting for use at rehearsals and by the time we came to shoot all the cast knew the sets very well indeed." (*Stringer.*)

Plaster can also be used to help solve the snow problems but in the snow sequences in *Fiddler on the Roof* marble dust was extensively used to simulate snow.

"We had a snow problem and had to resort to artificial marble dust. This type of 'snow' had been used before in *Doctor Zhivago* and *Alfred the Great.* Plaster does quite well also, especially on roofs. In Zagreb in the Kiev riot scene we laid tons of marble dust and instead of laying snow on very large

136

roof areas we resorted to a matte painting. Jewison very reluctantly agreed to do this but in the end it turned out very well. We used a hard black matte mask and had the paintings done in England by Ray Capel." (*Stringer.*)

Cement
Cement is another easy material to obtain and use and is particularly useful for floors and roads. Concrete can be moulded into blocks and further treated to give it age. The floor of the courtyard at Macbeth's castle was made in concrete which was ramped slightly at the junction with the walls to offset the hard line between the vertical and horizontal planes.

Paint Textures
One will often have to give strong textures to a wall or other vertical surface using paint or paper.

"There are a tremendous number of good techniques that studio painters have used over the years to get convincing aging and other interesting textures. For example, one can get a *lichen* effect by mixing sawdust with paint and then spraying it on to a receptive surface. One can get good wall textures by using multi-layers of paint thickened by various filler substances like Surfex, and then scraped down." (*Stringer.*)

Fibreglass
Of the more recent materials, fibreglass is perhaps the most flexible in that one can achieve almost all finishes and surfaces when using it.

"Elizabethan linen fold panelling can be reproduced very effectively in fibreglass or in vacuum formed plastic. It can be effectively grained, saving a great amount of carpentry and joinery work. By making only one mould of a panel one can reproduce it endlessly. Slight sags and open joints can be added when the panelling has been assembled.

"On more modern subjects great use can be made of formicas, aluminiums and fibreglass as well as vacuum moulding but the costs may sometimes be high." (*Stringer.*)

"Some of the more modern materials are extremely good—particularly fibreglass, but the trouble with them is the price. It is the budget that determines the nature of the set rather than the availability of materials. Prices have doubled in the last few years." (*Stoll.*)

When designing *Cromwell* John Stoll had to produce many suits of armour.

"Armour is made in fibreglass these days. The problem is the expense. A soldier's suit of armour may cost in the region of £200 and if you multiply that figure by the hundreds that are in a battle scene one can appreciate the need to find economic ways of achieving the same visual effect without incurring that kind of expense." (*Stoll.*)

Local Materials and Labour
Economies can be made when shooting on location if local labour is used in the preparation of locally available materials.

"Much of one's materials may be available from a local timber yard or plasterers. Using local materials can reduce one's expenditure considerably, especially when one can use local labour. On *Ryan's Daughter* the village was built with local stone by local labour. All our sets in *Fiddler on the Roof* were

Texture is enhanced by effective lighting. Decline and Fall. *Designed by Jonathan Barry.*

built of local materials. The Yugoslav construction teams were brilliant in the use of timber. They would saw up whole tree trunks from which we made all the bracing and framing timbers and we clad the exteriors with locally obtained re-worked old timbers. This saved an enormous amount of time. Normally we would have to burn and brush to age timber. We did the same in England by going to timber yards and finding as much old weathered timber as possible." (*Stringer.*)

Similar use of local labour was made when constructing the witches' shelter in *Macbeth*.

"While we were looking for a suitable location for this scene we came across a ruined cottage in a slate quarry. The structures were nothing like Gothic arches but by building on certain pieces of actual stone using local labour we were able to meet the requirements of the script under Polanski's direction *and* use an actual building made of local stone." (*Shingleton.*)

Texture

When deciding on the materials that will be used on a set one should take into account the kind of texture that one will be working for. Traditional materials like plaster are useful because they can be formed into any texture. Again, lighting is the key to bringing out the full value of the texture of a surface. Flat-on light can destroy a surface texture very easily and if the Designer wishes to give emphasis to a texture he should confer with the Lighting Cameraman to ensure the best lighting angles. Some of the points

138

Authentic copy of the Tudor "Opus Consutum" table-cloth, a form of "appliqué" needlework consisting of a felt motif stitched on to fine damask. The table-cloth was made by the Ladies Needlework Society in London to add authenticity to one scene in The Prince and the Pauper. *Designed by Michael Stringer.*

to look for are outlined by Michael Stringer:

"One should look for *keys* to texture in every set. One has to ask if the set is to be soft and feminine; silky; or deliberately vulgar with a multitude of satins and silks. On the other hand one can use hard or rough textures using stone, brick or earth. The setting of the story determines the texture but beyond the overall character of the story one can create smaller contrasts within the individual settings." (*Stringer.*)

Colour

Good colour stocks emerged during the period when realism was the predominating style in the cinema. Consequently, the use of colour is often limited to the enhancement of realism. With certain notable exceptions British and American cinema has tended to emphasise naturalism in colour rather than exploit its more emotive or expressive qualities. Colour is more often used to *describe* a scene rather than *comment* on it.

"Colours can be seen as an extension of character. There are some colours that can be used well dramatically—red for example. We used a red theme in a night club sequence in *A Shot in the Dark*. A murder is going to take place in this night club so we decided to use red as a strong contrast to the previous scene which was pale blue in colour. It is important in colour selection to ensure that the *tone* and *texture* of the colour relate together effectively." (*Stringer.*)

Roccoco opulence beautifully re-created by Nido Azzini for Death in Venice. *The salon of the Hôtel des Bains on the Lido at Venice was re-decorated for the film.*

One may have a very obvious colour to which one wishes to draw attention.

"In *Genevieve* we had two veteran cars, one red and black, the other one yellow belonging to the two main couples in the film. Immediately one could identify them apart from their shape.

"One of the biggest problems in the past was the fact that the early colour film stock process was rather un-subtle in its colour printing. Now, with better film stock we can get natural colours quite easily." (*Stringer.*)

Scott MacGregor in *Moon Zero Two* used colour in the costumes to help identify characters because as he says, characters in space tend to look alike. Colour in *Decline and Fall* was used as a witty comment on the heroine, her Rolls-Royce changing colour with her dress and in many of Scott MacGregor's horror films colour has to be used to underline the realism of the macabre situation. Perhaps when the vogue for realism is ended one will find colour used to exploit more of its expressive potential.

Chapter 9
The Designer and
Special Effects

The Designer assumes responsibility for the special effects or process work necessary in the production of a film. Indeed, the Designer should co-operate with the Special Effects department from the beginning since it is an integral part of the Art Department. Although the personnel in the Special Effects department are often highly specialist technicians they do not operate in a design vacuum. Their activities are initiated by the Designer in the light of the requirements of the script. The Bond films are classics in their use of effects and Ken Adam is a Designer who is capable of exploiting the full potential of the script in terms of special effects:

"The Bond films are quite terrifying from the point of view of the young person coming into the industry because they involve almost every aspect of film design. There are so many special effects; there is all the trick work; there is all the mechanical expertise that is so much a reflection of our era. At the same time there is the tongue in cheek feeling about so much of the action and of course I have to get this somehow into my design. It is exciting because one can use one's imagination more than in many other types of film. The problems, though, can be quite overpowering; all the gadgets (one is well into the field of engineering); plus all the set-up sketches and models. In terms of design content it would be comparable to an historical epic like *Cleopatra* or *Ben-Hur* but slightly ahead of time." (*Adam.*)

Of course most Designers will never be called upon to use such a complex range of effects in one film as Adam has done in the Bond series. But it is important for the Designer to understand the basic principles of effects and process photography and the potential of each method or technique. It is beyond the scope of this chapter to give a detailed analysis of the whole field of photographic effects. The subject will be covered fully in a later volume in this series.

During his initial reading of the script some of the action involved might well demand some kind of effect work or process photography and the Designer should discuss these sequences with the Director and Producer who may have their own ideas of how certain problems raised by the action should be solved. Some Directors do not like using special effects, preferring to do things as realistically as possible. The Producer, who has to find the money for the production, may consider some effects too costly and require the script to be changed or have other suggestions to make. In the end the factors that decide what effects if any will be used are: the Director's approach to the script; the Budget and other available resources; the Designer's concept of the final screen image. The Designer himself may have personal preferences with regard to technique and many factors will be at play in arriving at final decisions.

Glass Shots

The Designer may decide to utilise the glass shot when he needs to economise in the construction of architectural detail, perhaps when a building will stand in the background of the picture. By eliminating the need to build an extensive set the Designer can help the work of other technicians, for example the sound department, by giving them more flexibility in the placement of their equipment. In some films in which extensive building seems required without there being too much action the budget can be helped by eliminating the need for extensive and costly sets.

"When considering the reconstruction of the Guild Hall in London at the time of Henry VIII, the sheer cost of building up to forty feet would have been enormous for the one set which hadn't very much action in it. We decided that a glass painting could be used to give maximum effect to the establishing shot. We were thus able to paint the top twenty feet of the set on glass as well as all the foreground banners and the statue. The same technique was used for the exterior shot of Westminster Abbey. We needed a spectacular shot of the coronation being prepared. It was quite simple to set up the bottom quarter of the picture on the lot and paint in the rest. The two images have to be lined up in the Art Department first to choose the right lens and then project what is going to be painted on glass. An eight feet by six feet piece of glass is then put in front of the camera and the scenic painter paints in oils the top of the set. The benefit of this method is that one gets a direct composite picture that can be balanced for colour." (*Stringer.*)

The technique was also used by Michael Stringer for some of the backgrounds in *Fiddler on the Roof.*

"In *Fiddler* we used a hard black mask around the camera—the painting was put on glass afterwards. The film was then put through the camera once more and the two images were thus put together. Foreground glass painting does

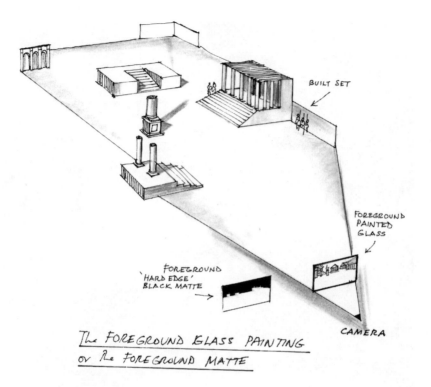

BUILT SET

FOREGROUND
PAINTED
GLASS

FOREGROUND
'HARD EDGE'
BLACK MATTE

CAMERA

The FOREGROUND GLASS PAINTING
or the FOREGROUND MATTE

143

Preparing a glass shot in the Guildhall scene in Walt Disney's Prince *and the* Pauper. *Designed by Michael Stringer.*

pay off since one can save the dupe." (*Stringer.*)

For the glass shot to be effective it has to be convincing in all its detail and there should be full preliminary discussions between the Designer, the Director and the Artist before work begins. The Designer will supply the Artist with very detailed sketches which will include all the action that will take place on that set.

144

TRAVELLING MATTE

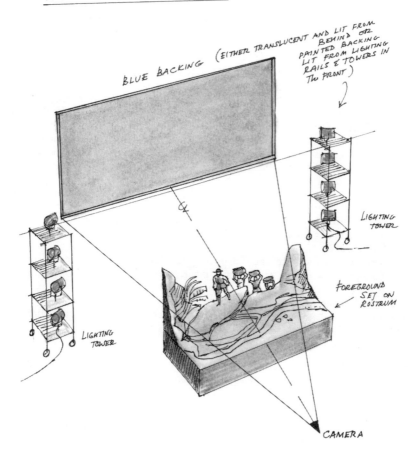

BLUE BACKING (EITHER TRANSLUCENT AND LIT FROM BEHIND OR PAINTED BACKING LIT FROM LIGHTING RAILS & TOWERS IN THE FRONT)

LIGHTING TOWER

LIGHTING TOWER

FOREGROUND SET ON ROSTRUM

CAMERA

Travelling Matte

The basic purpose of the Travelling Matte is to place a moving scene shot usually on location behind actors or action which takes place in the studio. The two sets of action are "married" during laboratory processing. During the printing stage a mask in the shape of the foreground action is used to prevent the background from "ghosting" through the foreground action.

Blue Screen Travelling Matte

The Blue Screen Travelling Matte process has two basic systems, both of them using a blue backing in front of which the foreground action takes place. The basic procedures for each system is as follows.

System A
1. The action is placed in front of a blue backing and is lit with normal studio lighting using colour negative stock.
2. By step painting with a black/white master positive recording only the blue colour in the scene a black/white positive results having clear background and black image.
3. The same procedure is followed recording only the red colours in the scene. The resulting positive has a clear image against a black background. By step printing the positive a high contrast dupe is produced with the action placed against a clear background.
4. The positive produced in Stage 2 is then printed in bi-pack with the dupe negative produced in Step 3 on to black/white high contrast stock.
   The foreground image is now seen as a clear area or "matte" against a black background. A black "matte" can then be printed against a clear background.
5. The two mattes are then printed with the foreground action positive (Stage 1) and the background positive giving the required composite image.

The fault with the process is that it tends to produce blue haloes or black lines around the foreground action. The Designer should also ensure that there are no deep blue colours in foreground costumes or props.

System B
Direct Matte
The set-up against the blue backing is essentially are same as in the above process except that the scene is lit with yellow light. The negative stock will show the foreground action blue against a yellow background. The negative is then printed on to black/white positive stock giving a black foreground matte against a clear background.

The background has meanwhile been photographed in a normal way using colour negative stock and a colour positive print is produced. The background positive print and the foreground matte are printed together in Bi-Pack to produce a black foreground matte against a colour positive background.

The foreground negative is printed using a yellow filter to give a yellow positive foreground against a black background.

The yellow foreground positive image and the positive background image are printed together to produce a composite negative.

The final composite print will show the normally lit foreground action against the location background quite convincingly.

Advantages
The haloes and black lines do not appear in this process; laboratory processing is relatively speedy; the background action can be shot at any time, and the time spent on setting up in the studio is relatively short.

146

Planning for Process Shots

If on reading the script the Designer anticipates having to use a process shot he will normally contact the camera department. The Designer will have to work out precisely what background footage will be required for each shot and he will supply the second unit with a very detailed set of continuity sketches.

"The content of the plates has to be spelled out quite clearly so that they will match up with studio action. Direction of movements, colours, and specific shot content all have to be carefully controlled. The cameramen will then fill in a report form specifying camera used, lens, and aperture, camera height etc." (*Shampan.*)

(A detailed account of the procedure for shooting background plates is to be found in "Practical Motion Picture Photography" compiled and edited by Russell Campbell in the Screen Textbook series published by The Tantivy Press.)

Back Projection

Back Projection is a system whereby foreground action takes place in front of a background image which has been projected on to a specially constructed screen. The projected background image may have been shot on location or indeed anywhere else that provides a suitable background image.

This old established system of producing a composite screen image has many advantages, not least is the fact that at a time when many Directors do not like the limitations of some process systems, Back Projections impose comparatively few restrictions on them in their direction of the actors. The camera can be moved and the actors can also move (unlike the Travelling Matte process, for example, which requires static "action.")

The Designer can put whatever is necessary in front of the back projection screen—it can be an actor, a prop, or a miniature. He will have to ensure that the background plates are shot to the precise requirements of the set-up that he has planned.

Backgrounds can either be moving plates shot by the second unit or they may be "still" shots taken with a five inch by four inch camera (see illustration).

Front Projection

Although the Front Projection system is also concerned with placing foreground action in front of a moving background plate, the method is more simple than the Back Projection system and offers advantages of flexibility and economy.

The system relies on a highly reflective screen placed behind the action, with the plate projector projecting its image on to the screen from the camera side of the screen. The set-up is as in the above illustration.

The two way mirror is set at a forty-five degree angle to both the camera and the plate projector. The projected image falls on the mirror and is reflected on to the screen lying behind the action. The screen, with its highly reflective surface, reflects the image back to the mirror. This transmits the light to the camera, which is placed to photograph the action.

It will be apparent that once the camera/projection system has been set up the camera becomes static since both have to maintain their precise relationship with the two way mirror. This is one of the system's disadvantages when compared with the back projection system, which allows camera mobility.

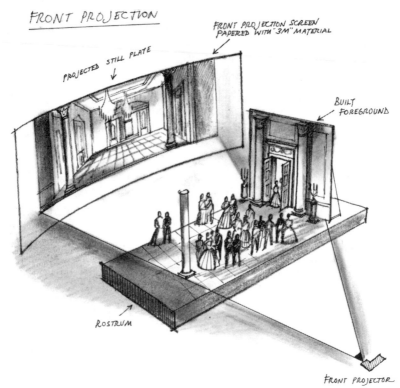

FRONT PROJECTION

PROJECTED STILL PLATE

FRONT PROJECTION SCREEN
PAPERED WITH "3M" MATERIAL

BUILT
FOREGROUND

ROSTRUM

FRONT PROJECTOR

Front projection. Lay-out for a typical set-up.

Another problem that may arise is that because of a certain amount of light loss inherent in any reflex system dark areas in the background plates will appear even darker. One should plan for even lighting without strong shade.

Ray Harryhausen, who has used both Back Projection and Front Projection systems for many years, discusses some of the problems he has met when using them:

"I have used Front Projection notably in *Beast from 20,000 Fathoms* and earlier in *Mighty Joe Young*. In this latter film made with Willis O'Brien it wasn't quite the same technique as one uses today because the beaded screen hadn't been invented. The main asset of Front Projection today is that one can get an enormous picture with very little light where with Rear Projection even to get a moderate size image one has to use a triple head in order to get enough light. One has to have three projectors projecting three images superimposed on one another. This is the only way to get a good sharp image.

"Another problem is that colour deteriorates each time it is reproduced. Present day systems are much better than they were in the mid-Fifties for

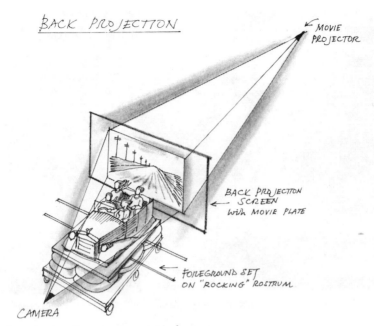

BACK PROJECTION

MOVIE
PROJECTOR

BACK PROJECTION
SCREEN
with MOVIE PLATE

FOREGROUND SET
ON "ROCKING" ROSTRUM

CAMERA

Back projection. Lay-out for a typical set-up.

example but there still is a tremendous loss of definition that sometimes bothers people. When one cuts to a special effects shot the image gets very grainy. This is one of the risks one takes with rear-projection systems." (*Harryhausen.*)

Miniatures
Miniatures are extremely detailed models of objects or people that can be used in a film to give convincing background detail, or they can be used in foreground action when for various reasons it is better to use a model than the real object or person; e.g. Ray Harryhausen had to use an articulated model of Raquel Welch for one scene in *One Million Years B.C.*

"Some of the models are built in clay—others in sponge rubber. Some are cast with the armature inserted afterwards. The model of Raquel Welch used in *One Million Years B.C.* moves in every joint—even the shoulders move. The model was used in the sequence of her being picked up by the Pterodactyl. Most of the models are made by me although sometimes I have somebody else to make them for me to my designs.

149

Where Eagles Dare *Designed by Peter Mullins. Ecktachrome still used as a reverse angle insert.*

Each joint has to be carefully made to give it friction and the skin (usually of rubber) has to be of the right flexibility and tension. The little horse we used in *Gwangi* was built so that one could see the ears move, it could even twitch them! The mouth opened and he could chew. The skin was real animal skin. The elephant in the same film was built because we couldn't find an eleven foot elephant and we had to animate those sequences. He could stand on his head and do all kinds of circus tricks and many people thought he was an actual performing elephant." (*Harryhausen.*)

Mechanical models are also very useful; cars, trains and even model aircraft can be used successfully in some circumstances, Syd Cain discusses his use of models in the film *Iron Daffodil*.

"Sometimes a shot is put in to help overcome a design problem. In *Iron Daffodil* I obviously cannot get a whole Panzer devision so I have perhaps to design a long shot in which the hero makes the point that we are looking at a whole division. In fact I may only have one or two full-size tanks which I can cut-in to in close-up; the rest of the division might be mock-ups or camouflaged other types. They then get attacked by a Stuka which will be a model. In the script there is an over the shoulder shot of the hero with the Stuka coming towards him—which would mean using a full-sized aeroplane. This would be impractical since the Stukas are very rare. One could convert another aircraft but this would cost money. So instead of doing an over-shoulder shot one could shoot an eyeline shot of what he sees. One can then use a seven foot radio-controlled model of the Stuka. On the screen the difference is hardly noticeable. It would be shot with a telephoto lens at two or three hundred feet. One can get as close as one needs to shoot without destroying the

150

Ray Harryhausen makes extensive use of models and miniatures in his superb films. Frame blow-up from Jason and the Argonauts. *Designed by Ray Harryhausen.*

illusion although one couldn't get too near the model of the pilot. Models tend to give themselves away by being too clean so it should be aged down. The other problem with models is the lighting but one can counter this by shooting outside." (*Cain.*)

In *The Iron Daffodil* Syd Cain has also had problems when building life size model tanks:

"Shooting inside a tank is quite tricky since we have to build it larger than life or we would never get our camera in. All the sides have to come away to enable us to include the different angles in the tank.

"We also had to decide whether to convert an existing tank or make a real one. In this film we will have to build a complete Matilda tank. There are only two Matilda tanks in existence and they are in a tank museum. This tank is virtually one of the stars of the picture so it is worth spending money to get the real thing. Of course it will have a modern engine so that it will not break down in the middle of a take and I also want it to go faster than the original version which could only reach six m.p.h. You can't hold on that speed or else people will start to yawn. We'll give it a maximum speed of about thirty m.p.h. Visually it will be an exact replica." (*Cain.*)

151

Complex perspectivised backing used in Where Eagles Dare. *Designed by Peter Mullins.*

Table Top Miniatures and Live-Action

Small models can be used effectively with live-action when the movements of the model and the actor are carefully rehearsed. Ray Harryhausen describes how he sets up such a sequence.

"The action that will eventually involve process techniques is like shadow boxing. The whole thing has to be carefully arranged to take the process shots into account. After this stage has been completed we take what we have got into a small studio and set up our table top miniature. Sometimes we will project the live action on to a screen behind the model, re-photographing the model and live action frame by frame; other times one shoots the model against a blue backing.

"The timing of the shots can be complicated especially when one has more than one figure. When we had seven skeletons duelling with three men every-thing had to be synchronised so that when a sword came down it wouldn't just disappear into nothing. In sequences such as that we rehearse with stand-ins taking the place of the animated figures. It is choreographed like a ballet so that when we take the stand-in out of the action the live figure then 'shadow boxes.' The skeletons are then put in place to fit in with the live action." (*Harryhausen.*)

The REDUCTION PLATE AND MATTE PAINTING

The COMPOSITE PICTURE

FULL APERTURE PLATE OF BUILT SET WITH ACTION AREA
TO BE REDUCED DOWN AND MATTED INTO PAINTING

MATTE PAINTING SHOWING AREA FOR REDUCTION
PLATE OF BUILT SET

The COMPOSITE PICTURE

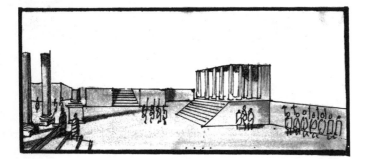

The BUILT SET

The FOREGROUND MINIATURE SET
or The FOREGROUND GLASS PAINTING
or The MATTE PAINTING

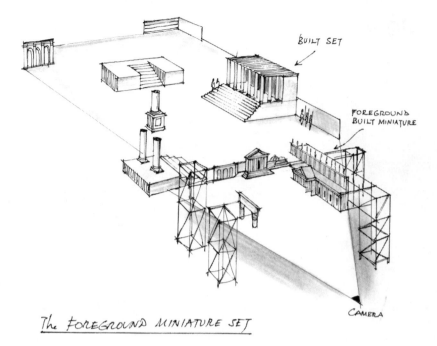

BUILT SET

FOREGROUND
BUILT MINIATURE

CAMERA

The FOREGROUND MINIATURE SET

Hanging Miniatures

Miniatures placed between the camera and the "normal" set so as to appear on screen as part of the normal set are termed hanging miniatures (see illustration). Although they often serve a similar purpose to the glass painting they have an enhanced, three-dimensional quality that gives a more acceptable and convincing illusion.

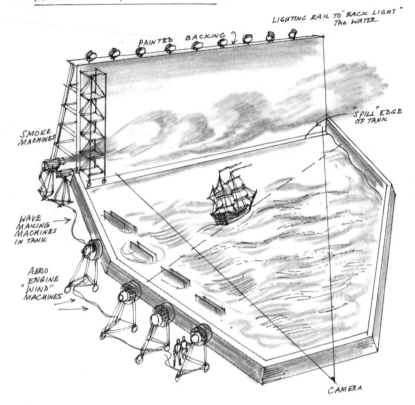

The Studio Exterior Tank

Some film studios have large exterior water tanks primarily for model ship work. They are usually four feet deep with a feather edge horizon spill edge set twelve feet from the backing. Wave-making machines can be set up inside the water tank for making waves in conjunction with wind machines and smoke machines for moving clouds. Being miniature the film is shot at speed producing a slight slow motion effect, and the size of the water particles breaking up does not appear too unnatural. The miniature vessels are designed in the Art

Department and are towed across the tank by underwater runners, and sometimes frogmen inside the miniature vessels steer them. The tank can also be used for shots of full-size vessels if carefully planned—but usually only sections of full-size vessels can be used—depending on the size. Most studios also have smaller tanks in some of the stages which can also be used for staircase wells. The "Silent" Stage (Stage H) at Shepperton has a concrete wall four feet all round the stage and a concrete floor so that the entire stage (240 feet by 120 feet) can be turned into one large interior water tank. Interior tanks like this can be extremely useful for controlled interior shooting for storm sequences in *The Guns of Navarone* or the misty river sequence in *Lord Jim.*

Examples of Costume Design to study:

Margaret Furse	*Anne of the Thousand Days, Becket, Greyfriars Bobby, Mary Queen of Scots, In Search of the Castaways.*
Jocelyn Rickards	*Blow Up, Ryan's Daughter, Alfred the Great.*
Anthony Mendelson	*Oh! What a Lovely War, Young Winston.*
Elizabeth Haffenden and Joan Bridge	*Fiddler on the Roof, A Man for All Seasons.*
Phyllis Dalton	*Lawrence of Arabia, Ben-Hur.*
Jocelyn Herbert	*Tom Jones.*
Lila de Nobili	*The Charge of the Light Brigade.*
Piero Tosi	*Death in Venice.*
Ann Roth	*Midnight Cowboy.*
Irene Sharaff	*The King and I, West Side Story, Julius Caesar.*
Roger Furse	*Hamlet, Henry V.*

Examples of Film Design to study:

John Bryan	*Great Expectations, Oliver Twist, Blanche Fury, Becket.*
Vincent Korda	*Things to Come, Rembrandt, An Ideal Husband.*
Tom Morahan	*Jamaica Inn, Captain Hornblower.*
Carmen Dillon	*Henry V, The Importance of Being Earnest, The Go-Between.*
John Box	*Lawrence of Arabia, Doctor Zhivago, Oliver!, Nicholas and Alexandra.*
Terence March	*Lawrence of Arabia, Doctor Zhivago, Oliver!, Scrooge, Mary Queen of Scots.*
Paul Sheriff	*Henry V, Moulin Rouge.*
Tony Masters	*2001: A Space Odyssey.*
Ken Adam	*Dr. No, Thunderball, Dr. Strangelove, You Only Live Twice.*
Robert Boyle	*Fiddler on the Roof, Marnie, The Thomas Crown Affair, North by Northwest, The Birds.*
John Howell	*The Prime of Miss Jean Brodie, Swiss Family Robinson.*
Alexander Trauner	*Les Enfants du Paradis, The Nun's Story, Rififi, Irma La Douce.*
Richard Day	*On the Waterfront, On Your Toes.*
Maurice Carter	*Becket.*
Peter Murton	*The Lion in Winter.*
John de Cuir	*The King and I, Cleopatra, Hello Dolly!*
Richard Sylbert	*Who's Afraid of Virginia Woolf?*
Boris Leven	*West Side Story, The Sound of Music.*
Lazar Meerson	*La Kermesse Héroïque.*

Alex Vetchinsky	*Jane Eyre, Morning Departure, Hungry Hill, A Night to Remember.*
Stephen Grimes	*Ryan's Daughter, Freud.*
L. P. Williams	*Brief Encounter.*
Andre Andrejew	*Anna Karenina.*
Hein Heckroth	*The Red Shoes.*
Alfred Junge	*Black Narcissus, A Matter of Life and Death.*
Oliver Messel	*The Queen of Spades.*
Michael Relph	*Saraband for Dead Lovers.*
David Rawnsley	*In Which We Serve.*
Roger Furse	*Hamlet.*
Sergei Eisenstein	*Alexander Nevsky, Ivan the Terrible.*
Edward Carrick	*The Blue Lagoon.*
Norman Arnold	*Hue and Cry.*
Geoffrey Drake	*Young Winston, The Bridge on the River Kwai, The Guns of Navarone.*
Don Ashton	*Oh! What a Lovely War, The Bridge on the River Kwai.*

Notes on Contributors

1. Michael Stringer. Born 1925, Singapore. Joined Norman Arnold's staff as junior draughtsman after demob from RAF in 1946, and after several years became his assistant on *The Galloping Major* (1951). Subsequently became Assistant Art Director on *Chance of a Lifetime;* first film as Art Director with Government-sponsored Group 3 on Lewis Gilbert's *Time Gentlemen Please!* After several more Group 3 films, worked on *Genevieve,* subsequently becoming a Rank Contact Art Director on *The Captain's Table, Sea Fury,* etc. Chief films since then: *The Sundowners, In Search of the Castaways, 633 Squadron, A Shot in the Dark, Return from the Ashes, Cast a Giant Shadow, Inspector Clouseau, Young Cassidy, Casino Royale, Alfred the Great, Fiddler on the Roof, Alice's Adventures in Wonderland.* Also work in theatre (e.g. Brecht's "Galileo" at the Mermaid).

2. Peter Mullins. Born 1931, London. Entered industry in 1947 as a scenic artist. Much work in TV on series such as "Robin Hood", "William Tell" and "The Invisible Man". Chief films since 1964: *King and Country, Alfie, The Spy with a Cold Nose, The Man Outside, A Home of Your Own, Pretty Polly, Where Eagles Dare, The Most Dangerous Man in the World, The Last Valley, Puppet on a Chain, Zee & Co., Steptoe and Son.*

3. John Stoll. Born 1913, London. Entered industry in 1946. Main films: *The Camp on Blood Island, The Greengage Summer, Lawrence of Arabia, The Running Man, The 7th. Dawn, The Collector, How I Won the War, A Twist of Sand, Hannibal Brooks, Cromwell, Living Free, The Darwin Adventure.*

4. Scott MacGregor. Born 1914, Roslin, near Edinburgh, Scotland. Stage designer and scenic artist before entering industry in 1941 as assistant to Edward Carrick (*Target for Tonight, Western Approaches*). With the Crown Film Unit until 1950 (Art Director from 1946). Freelance ever since. Chief films: *Children on Trial, Steps of the Ballet, Four Men in Prison, Sonja Henie in London, The Secret, The Day They Robbed the Bank of England, The Criminal, Oscar Wilde, Cleopatra, Day of the Triffids, The Man Who Finally Died, Khartoum, Sumuru, The Vengeance of Fu Manchu, Baby Love, Moon Zero Two, Taste the Blood of Dracula, Scars of Dracula, Burke and Hare, Blood from the Mummy's Tomb, On the Buses, Vampire Circus, Straight on Till Morning, Frankenstein and the Monster from Hell.*

5. Ray Harryhausen. Born 1920, Los Angeles. Educated L.A. City College and U.C.L.A. After graduating, worked with George Pal on the animated *Puppetoons.* Following War service, taken on by Willis (*King Kong*) O'Brien as his assistant. 1949: feature *début* on *Mighty Joe Young.* Inventor of Super Dynamation, Dynamation 90 and Dynamation. 1953: *The Beast from 20,000 Fathoms.* Dynamation process really came to fore with his partnership with Charles H. Schneer. Films since then: *It Came from beneath the Sea* (1955; first in process), *The Earth vs Flying Saucers, The Animal World* (dinosaur sequence, with Willis O'Brien), *Twenty Million Miles to Earth, The 7th. Voy-*

age of Sinbad. The Three Worlds of Gulliver, Mysterious Island, Jason and the Argonauts, The First Men in the Moon, The Valley of Gwangi, One Million Years B.C. (in Giant Panamation), *Sinbad's Golden Voyage.* Has his own specially-equipped studio at Slough, Buckinghamshire.

6. **Ken Adam.** Born 1921, Berlin. Came to England in 1934. Entered industry in 1947 as a draughtsman (*Queen of Spades,* etc.). 1948–53: Assistant (*Obsession, Star of India*) and Associate (*The Crimson Pirate*) Art Director. 1956–59: full Art Director (*Around the World in Eighty Days*—European scenes, *The Angry Hills*). Since 1959 Production Designer on *The Rough and the Smooth, In the Nick, Let's Get Married, The Trials of Oscar Wilde, Sodom and Gomorrah, Dr. No, In the Cool of the Day, Dr. Strangelove, Woman of Straw, Goldfinger, The Ipcress File, Thunderball, You Only Live Twice, Chitty Chitty Bang Bang, Goodbye Mr. Chips, The Owl and the Pussycat, Diamonds Are Forever, Sleuth.*

7. **Ted Marshall.** Born 1917, Wiltshire. Educated at Malvern College. After school, trained and qualified as an architect, practising this profession until the Forties. Entered industry at Denham as a draughtsman at the request of an Art Director ex-colleague. After work in Art Department, first chance as assistant to Art Director Ralph Brinton on *The Chiltern Hundreds.* Others: *Trottie True, Scrooge,* etc. Since 1958 has made several films with Woodfall. Films since then: *Room at the Top, The Entertainer, Saturday Night and Sunday Morning, A Taste of Honey, The Quare Fellow, The Loneliness of the Long Distance Runner, Tom Jones, The Girl with Green Eyes, The Pumpkin Eater, The Uncle, Life at the Top, The Spy Who Came in from the Cold, Marat-Sade, Charlie Bubbles, The Charge of the Light Brigade, The Birthday Party, Some Girls Do, The Executioner, Macho Callahan, The Triple Echo.*

8. **Syd Cain.** Became Assistant Art Director in mid-Fifties (*Cockleshell Heroes, The Inn of the Sixth Happiness, The World of Susie Wong, Our Man in Havana*). Since 1962, Art Director/Production Designer on following films: *Lolita, Summer Holiday, Dr. No, The Road to Hong Kong, Hot Enough for June, Call Me Bwana, From Russia with Love, The High Bright Sun, Mister Moses, The Amorous Adventures of Moll Flanders, A Funny Thing Happened on the Way to the Forum, Fahrenheit 451, Billion Dollar Brain, On Her Majesty's Secret Service, Murphy's War, Frenzy, Live and Let Die.*

9. **Jonathan (John) Barry.** Born 1935, London. Qualified as architect at Kingston School of Art in 1959. Entered industry in 1961 at Pinewood as draughtsman on *Cleopatra.* Thereafter worked on various films and TV series as draughtsman, set dresser, etc. 1964: became assistant to Elliot Scott, supervising Art Director at M-G-M British Studios. First film as a designer: *Decline and Fall . . . of a Birdwatcher.* Work since then includes *Kelly's Heroes, A Clockwork Orange, Phase Four, Little Prince.* (Mr. Barry's real name is John; his earlier use of Jonathan was to avoid confusion with the film music composer.)

10. Wilfrid Shingleton. Born 1914, London. Educated at Cardinal Vaughan School, Kensington. Entered industry in 1931 with RKO at Ealing. Main films since 1951: *The African Queen, Hobson's Choice, A Kid for Two Farthings, The Key, Trouble in the Sky, For the Love of Mike, Tunes of Glory, Waltz of the Toreadors, The Innocents, Stolen Hours, Judith, Promise Her Anything, The Blue Max, Sebastian, Dance of the Vampires, Prudence and the Pill, Macbeth.*

11. Jack Shampan. Born London. Prior to Second World War worked for an interior decorating firm, setting up his own business after War. Due to restrictions forced to look for other work, and entered industry at Ealing Studios as a senior draughtsman, working on *Saraband for Dead Lovers, Kind Hearts and Coronets, The Lavender Hill Mob,* and others. Became Art Director, working on three of director Sidney Hayers's films—*Circus of Horrors* (1960), *Payroll, Night of the Eagle.* Joined M-G-M British as Art Director on *Private Potter* and others. Subsequent film work on *Modesty Blaise* and *Finders Keepers.* Important TV work on "Danger Man" (early episodes) and "The Prisoner" (all).

12. Alan Withy. Born 1923, London. Studied Art at Goldsmiths College, 1939–42. After subsequent experience in engineering and draughtsmanship, entered industry in 1947 to work in Art Department on *The Red Shoes.* After series of films at Pinewood, resigned in 1952 to work freelance (e.g. *Conchita*). Until 1956 worked as either draughtsman or Assistant Art Director. Films since then: *Davy, Barnacle Bill, Nowhere to Go, The Scapegoat, The Siege of Pinchgut, The Night Apart, Too Hot to Handle, Green Helmet, Secret Partner, Go to Blazes, The Lion, This Sporting Life, Girl in the Headlines, The Family Way, O Lucky Man!, Escort Service* (British half only of Italian co-prod.). Since 1959 very active in commercials, having worked on more than 250 to date.

Index

(Designers quoted, films discussed, and general subjects are indexed. Italics refer to illustrations.)

164